Mathematica Data Visualization

Create and prototype interactive data visualizations using Mathematica

Nazmus Saquib

BIRMINGHAM - MUMBAI

Mathematica Data Visualization

First published: September 2014

Production reference: 1180914

Published by Packt Publishing Ltd.
Livery Place
35 Livery Street
Birmingham B3 2PB, UK.

ISBN 978-1-78328-299-9

www.packtpub.com

Credits

Author
Nazmus Saquib

Reviewers
Roger J. Brown
Wenjun Deng
Kristjan Kannike

Commissioning Editor
Akram Hussain

Acquisition Editor
Mohammad Rizvi

Content Development Editor
Anila Vincent

Technical Editors
Venu Manthena
Aman Preet Singh

Copy Editors
Sayanee Mukherjee
Alfida Paiva

Project Coordinator
Neha Bhatnagar

Proofreaders
Martin Diver
Maria Gould

Indexers
Monica Ajmera Mehta
Tejal Soni

Production Coordinator
Manu Joseph

Cover Work
Manu Joseph

About the Author

Nazmus Saquib is a researcher at the MIT Media Lab in Cambridge, MA, where he works on data visualization, machine learning, and social computing projects. He has a bachelor's degree in Physics and a master's degree in Computational Engineering and Applied Mathematics. Saquib has been programming 3D games since middle school. As a result, he has developed and maintains a keen interest in game engines, graphics, and visualization. Throughout his academic years, he worked on a wide range of research projects, including acoustics, particle physics, augmented reality, social data mining, and uncertainty quantification. Saquib is also interested in the applications of creative computing in education and social welfare.

About the Reviewers

Roger J. Brown is the President of IMOJIM, Inc., one of the oldest commercial investment firms in San Diego, which is now completing its fifth decade. His experience includes numerous consulting and expert witness assignments, and ownership or origination of loans on various properties in seven states of the US. He obtained his PhD in Finance from Pennsylvania State University in 2000, writing his dissertation on Levy-stable (non-normal, and heavy-tailed) return distributions. He is the author of *Private Real Estate Investment*, published by *Academic Press*, which is now in its second edition.

Wenjun Deng is a Computational Physicist at Princeton University and Princeton Plasma Physics Laboratory. He obtained his BS from the University of Science and Technology of China in 2006, and his PhD in Physics from the University of California, Irvine in 2012. His research interests include modeling and simulations of fusion plasmas and laser-excited high-energy-density plasmas. To comprehensively understand these complex plasmas, which are composed of a huge number of electrically charged ions and electrons as well as electromagnetic fields, is one of the most difficult challenges in human history. To advance the frontier of this field, he works with his collaborators to develop, debug, optimize, and run large-scale simulations on world-leading high-performance computing facilities. By carefully analyzing and visualizing the simulation data, he is able to dig out the underlying physical principles and thus able to predict and optimize the behaviors of these plasmas in experiments.

> I would like to thank my wife Liang for her continuous encouragement and support.

Kristjan Kannike is a Theoretical Particle Physicist at the National Institute of Chemical Physics and Biophysics in Estonia. He uses Mathematica daily to simulate and visualize models of high-energy physics.

www.PacktPub.com

Support files, eBooks, discount offers, and more

You might want to visit www.PacktPub.com for support files and downloads related to your book.

Did you know that Packt offers eBook versions of every book published, with PDF and ePub files available? You can upgrade to the eBook version at www.PacktPub.com and as a print book customer, you are entitled to a discount on the eBook copy. Get in touch with us at service@packtpub.com for more details.

At www.PacktPub.com, you can also read a collection of free technical articles, sign up for a range of free newsletters and receive exclusive discounts and offers on Packt books and eBooks.

http://PacktLib.PacktPub.com

Do you need instant solutions to your IT questions? PacktLib is Packt's online digital book library. Here, you can access, read and search across Packt's entire library of books.

Why subscribe?

- Fully searchable across every book published by Packt
- Copy and paste, print and bookmark content
- On demand and accessible via web browser

Free access for Packt account holders

If you have an account with Packt at www.PacktPub.com, you can use this to access PacktLib today and view nine entirely free books. Simply use your login credentials for immediate access.

Table of Contents

Preface   **1**

Chapter 1: Visualization as a Tool to Understand Data   **7**

The importance of visualization   **9**

Types of datasets   **11**
Tables   12
Scalar fields   12
Time series   14
Graphs   14
Text   15
Cartographic data   15

Mathematica as a tool for visualization   **15**

Getting started with Mathematica   **17**
Creating and selecting cells   17
Evaluating a cell   18
Suppressing output from a cell   18
Cell formatting   18
Commenting   19
Aborting evaluation   19

Upcoming chapters   **19**

Further reading   **20**

Summary   **20**

Chapter 2: Dissecting Data Using Mathematica   **21**

Data structures and core languages   **21**
Introducing lists   22
Nested lists   23
Matrices   23
Constructing lists programmatically   24
Accessing elements from a list   27
Applying set operations on lists   29

Functions and conditionals	32
Declaring and using functions	32
Conditionals	33
Further core language	34
Data importing and basic plots	**34**
Importing data into Mathematica	34
SetDirectory[] and NotebookDirectory[]	35
Loading the dataset	35
Basic plotting functions	36
ListPlot	36
Styling our plots	39
Plot legends	41
3D point plots	43
Log plots	44
Further reading	**46**
Summary	**47**
Chapter 3: Time Series and Scientific Visualization	**49**
Periodic patterns in time series	**50**
Sector charts	51
Simulating Internet activity	52
SectorChart and its options	54
Interactive visualization of financial data	**57**
The DateListPlot function	58
Adding interactivity – preliminaries	60
Intermission – Graphics and Show	61
Adding interactivity – Dynamic and Refresh	63
Isocontour and molecular visualization	**64**
Introduction to isocontours	65
Example project – protein molecule visualization	67
Loading and visualizing the protein molecule	69
Preparing the isocontour plots	72
Adding interactivity – manipulate	73
Isosurface and styling	74
Thinking like a visualization scientist – isovalue analysis	76
Further reading	**77**
Summary	**78**
Chapter 4: Statistical and Information Visualization	**79**
Statistical visualization	**80**
The swiss bank notes dataset	81
Histograms and charts	82
Histogram	82
PairedHistogram	84
Histogram3D	85
PieChart	86

BubbleChart	87
Choosing appropriate plots	88
A glimpse of high-dimensional data	89
Similarity maps	89
Projecting information to low dimensions	90
Visualizing genuine and counterfeit clusters	90
Similarity map for smaller datasets	92
Things that can (and will) go wrong	94
Text visualization	**96**
A modified word cloud	97
Cleaning the data	98
The basic algorithm	98
Code and explanation	99
Graphs and networks	**102**
A basic graph visualization	102
Representing graphs in Mathematica	102
Visualizing the Les Misérables network	103
Highlighting centrality measures	103
Other graph layouts	105
3D layouts	106
Chord diagrams	106
Code and explanation	108
Tweaking the visualization	110
Further reading	**112**
Summary	**113**
Chapter 5: Maps and Aesthetics	**115**
Map visualization	**115**
The GeoGraphics package	116
A map of our current location	116
Plotting a path on the map	117
Interactivity in GeoGraphics	118
Anatomy of a map visualization engine	119
The visual interface	120
Code and explanation	121
Aesthetics in visualization	**124**
Choosing the right color map	124
The rainbow color map is misleading	125
Understanding hue and luminance	125
Some better color maps	126
Designing the right interface	126
Deploying Mathematica visualizations	**127**
Looking forward	**128**
Further reading	**128**
Summary	**128**
Index	**129**

Preface

Mathematica Data Visualization was written with one goal in mind — teaching the reader how to write interactive visualization programs seamlessly using Mathematica. Mathematica is the programming language of choice for many data analysts, mathematicians, scientists, engineers, and business analysts. It offers a powerful suite of data analysis and data mining packages, along with a very rich data visualization framework for its users.

After reading this book and working with the code examples provided, you will be proficient in building your own interactive data visualizations. You will have a good understanding of the different kinds of data that you may encounter as a data visualization expert, along with a solid foundation on the techniques of visualizing such data using Mathematica.

Whenever needed, this book teaches the essential theory behind any advanced concept, so a beginner in data visualization will not feel uncomfortable tackling the material. Other than traditional plots, this book teaches how to build advanced visualizations from scratch, such as chord diagrams, maps, protein molecule visualizations, and so on.

What this book covers

Chapter 1, Visualization as a Tool to Understand Data, introduces the reader to the world of data visualization. The importance of visualization is discussed, along with the description of different datasets that will be covered.

Chapter 2, Dissecting Data Using Mathematica, gives a short introduction to Mathematica programming in the context of data analysis and operations. It also introduces the readers to basic plots.

Chapter 3, *Time Series and Scientific Visualization*, deals with time series and scalar fields, detailing some methods of visualizing these types of data in Mathematica.

Chapter 4, *Statistical and Information Visualization*, teaches some methods of statistical and information visualization using several mini projects.

Chapter 5, *Maps and Aesthetics*, develops a map visualization using a geographic shape file. Some essential data visualization aesthetics are also discussed.

What you need for this book

You will require a computer with an installation of the latest version (10) of Mathematica. The notebooks were tested only with Versions 9 and 10. There are a small number of functions that are only present in Version 10, but almost all of the code listings will work in Versions 8 and 9 otherwise. The codes will work with both the student and Pro versions. If you do not have access to Mathematica, you can still view the code and interact with the visualizations using the freely downloadable CDF player from the Wolfram Mathematica website (http://www.wolfram.com/cdf-player/).

Who this book is for

This book is aimed at people who are familiar with basic programming and high school mathematics, and are enthusiastic to learn about data visualization and Mathematica. It does not assume any prior knowledge of advanced data analysis or statistical techniques. Familiarity with a programming language may prove to be useful, but it is not essential. For beginners in Mathematica, *Chapter 2*, *Dissecting Data Using Mathematica*, provides a short primer on the essentials of Mathematica programming. Readers who are already familiar with Mathematica may skip the first half of *Chapter 2*, *Dissecting Data Using Mathematica*.

Conventions

In this book, you will find a number of styles of text that distinguish between different kinds of information. Here are some examples of these styles, and an explanation of their meaning.

Code words in text, database table names, folder names, filenames, file extensions, pathnames, dummy URLs, user input, and Twitter handles are shown as follows: "The EdgeForm[None] function is used to ask Graphics to not render the polygon boundaries."

A block of code is set as follows:

```
SetDirectory[ NotebookDirectory[] ]
shpdat = Import["data/usa_state_shapefile.shp", "Data"]
names = shpdat[[1, 4, 2, 2, 2]];
polys = "Geometry" /. shpdat[[1]]
filenames = Table["data/usgs_state_" <> ToString[i] <> ".csv", {i,
2001, 2010}]
```

When we wish to draw your attention to a particular part of a code block, the relevant lines or items are set in bold:

```
SectorChart[{data1, data2, …}, options]
```

New terms and **important words** are shown in bold. Words that you see on the screen, in menus or dialog boxes for example, appear in the text like this: "The surface will represent the points in 3D space that has the same potential, the potential value of interest being selectable from the drop-down menu named **Contour**."

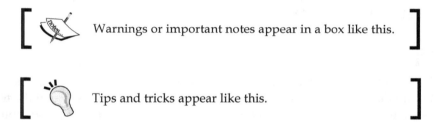

Warnings or important notes appear in a box like this.

Tips and tricks appear like this.

Reader feedback

Feedback from our readers is always welcome. Let us know what you think about this book—what you liked or may have disliked. Reader feedback is important for us to develop titles that you really get the most out of.

To send us general feedback, simply send an e-mail to feedback@packtpub.com, and mention the book title via the subject of your message.

If there is a topic that you have expertise in and you are interested in either writing or contributing to a book, see our author guide on www.packtpub.com/authors.

Customer support

Now that you are the proud owner of a Packt book, we have a number of things to help you to get the most from your purchase.

Downloading the example code

You can download the example code files for all Packt books you have purchased from your account at http://www.packtpub.com. If you purchased this book elsewhere, you can visit http://www.packtpub.com/support and register to have the files e-mailed directly to you.

Downloading the color images of this book

We also provide you a PDF file that has color images of the screenshots/diagrams used in this book. The color images will help you better understand the changes in the output. You can download this file from: http://www.packtpub.com/sites/default/files/downloads/29990T_coloredimages.pdf.

Errata

Although we have taken every care to ensure the accuracy of our content, mistakes do happen. If you find a mistake in one of our books—maybe a mistake in the text or the code—we would be grateful if you would report this to us. By doing so, you can save other readers from frustration and help us improve subsequent versions of this book. If you find any errata, please report them by visiting http://www.packtpub.com/submit-errata, selecting your book, clicking on the **errata submission form** link, and entering the details of your errata. Once your errata are verified, your submission will be accepted and the errata will be uploaded on our website, or added to any list of existing errata, under the Errata section of that title. Any existing errata can be viewed by selecting your title from http://www.packtpub.com/support.

Piracy

Piracy of copyright material on the Internet is an ongoing problem across all media. At Packt, we take the protection of our copyright and licenses very seriously. If you come across any illegal copies of our works, in any form, on the Internet, please provide us with the location address or website name immediately so that we can pursue a remedy.

Please contact us at copyright@packtpub.com with a link to the suspected pirated material.

We appreciate your help in protecting our authors, and our ability to bring you valuable content.

Questions

You can contact us at questions@packtpub.com if you are having a problem with any aspect of the book, and we will do our best to address it.

1
Visualization as a Tool to Understand Data

In the last few decades, the quick growth in the volume of information we produce and the capacity of digital information storage have opened a new door for data analytics. We have moved on from the age of terabytes to that of petabytes and exabytes. Traditional data analysis is now augmented with the term *big data analysis*, and computer scientists are pushing the bounds for analyzing this huge sea of data using statistical, computational, and algorithmic techniques.

Along with the size, the types and categories of data have also evolved. Along with the typical and popular data domain in Computer Science (text, image, and video), graphs and various categorical data that arise from Internet interactions have become increasingly interesting to analyze. With the advances in computational methods and computing speed, scientists nowadays produce an enormous amount of numerical simulation data that has opened up new challenges in the field of Computer Science.

Simulation data tends to be structured and clean, whereas data collected or scraped from websites can be quite unstructured and hard to make sense of. For example, let's say we want to analyze some blog entries in order to find out which blogger gets more follows and referrals from other bloggers. This is not as straightforward as getting some friends' information from social networking sites. Blog entries consist of text and HTML tags; thus, a combination of text analytics and tag parsing, coupled with a careful observation of the results would give us our desired outcome.

Regardless of whether the data is simulated or empirical, the key word here is observation. In order to make intelligent observations, data scientists tend to follow a certain pipeline. The data needs to be acquired and cleaned to make sure that it is ready to be analyzed using existing tools. Analysis may take the route of visualization, statistics, and algorithms, or a combination of any of the three. Inference and refining the analysis methods based on the inference is an iterative process that needs to be carried out several times until we think that a set of hypotheses is formed, or a clear question is asked for further analysis, or a question is answered with enough evidence.

Visualization is a very effective and perceptive method to make sense of our data. While statistics and algorithmic techniques provide good insights about data, an effective visualization makes it easy for anyone with little training to gain beautiful insights about their datasets. The power of visualization resides not only in the ease of interpretation, but it also reveals visual trends and patterns in data, which are often hard to find using statistical or algorithmic techniques. It can be used during any step of the data analysis pipeline—validation, verification, analysis, and inference—to aid the data scientist.

How have you visualized your data recently? If you still have not, it is okay, as this book will teach you exactly that. However, if you had the opportunity to play with any kind of data already, I want you to take a moment and think about the techniques you used to visualize your data so far. Make a list of them.

Done? Do you have 2D and 3D plots, histograms, bar charts, and pie charts in the list? If yes, excellent! We will learn how to style your plots and make them more interactive using Mathematica. Do you have chord diagrams, graph layouts, word cloud, parallel coordinates, isosurfaces, and maps somewhere in that list? If yes, then you are already familiar with some modern visualization techniques, but if you have not had the chance to use Mathematica as a data visualization language before, we will explore how visualization prototypes can be built seamlessly in this software using very little code.

The aim of this book is to teach a Mathematica beginner the data-analysis and visualization powerhouse built into Mathematica, and at the same time, familiarize the reader with some of the modern visualization techniques that can be easily built with Mathematica. We will learn how to load, clean, and dissect different types of data, visualize the data using Mathematica's built-in tools, and then use the Mathematica graphics language and interactivity functions to build prototypes of a modern visualization.

In this chapter, we will look at a few simple examples that demonstrate the importance of data visualization. We will then discuss the types of datasets that we will encounter over the course of this book, and learn about the Mathematica interface to get ourselves warmed up for coding.

The importance of visualization

Visualization has a broad definition, and so does data. The cave paintings drawn by our ancestors can be argued as visualizations as they convey historical data through a visual medium. Map visualizations were commonly used in wars since ancient times to discuss the past, present, and future states of a war, and to come up with new strategies. Astronomers in the 17th century were believed to have built the first visualization of their statistical data. In the 18th century, William Playfair invented many of the popular graphs we use today (line, bar, circle, and pie charts). Therefore, it appears as if many, since ancient times, have recognized the importance of visualization in giving some meaning to data.

To demonstrate the importance of visualization in a simple mathematical setting, consider fitting a line to a given set of points. Without looking at the data points, it would be unwise to try to fit them with a model that seemingly lowers the error bound. It should also be noted that sometimes, the data needs to be changed or transformed to the correct form that allows us to use a particular tool. Visualizing the data points ensures that we do not fall into any trap. The following screenshot shows the visualization of a polynomial as a circle:

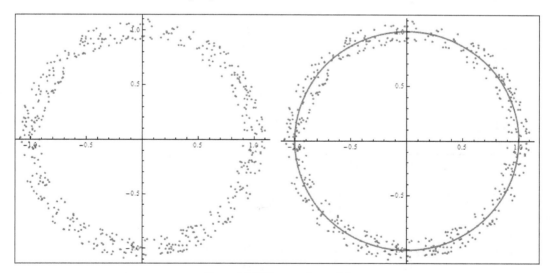

Figure 1.1 Fitting a polynomial

In figure 1.1, the points are distributed around a circle. Imagine we are given these points in a Cartesian space (orthogonal x and y coordinates), and we are asked to fit a simple linear model. There is not much benefit if we try to fit these points to any polynomial in a Cartesian space; what we really need to do is change the parameter space to polar coordinates. A 1-degree polynomial in polar coordinate space (essentially a circle) would nicely fit these points when they are converted to polar coordinates, as shown in figure 1.1. Visualizing the data points in more complicated but similar situations can save us a lot of trouble. The following is a screenshot of Anscombe's quartet:

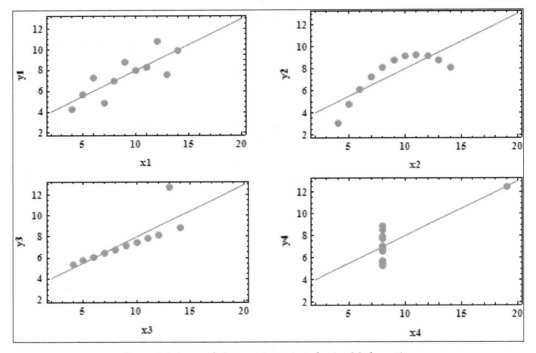

Figure 1.2 Anscombe's quartet, generated using Mathematica

Downloading the color images of this book

We also provide you a PDF file that has color images of the screenshots/diagrams used in this book. The color images will help you better understand the changes in the output. You can download this file from: https://www.packtpub.com/sites/default/files/downloads/2999OT_coloredimages.PDF.

Anscombe's quartet (figure 1.2), named after the statistician Francis Anscombe, is a classic example of how simple data visualization like plotting can save us from making wrong statistical inferences. The quartet consists of four datasets that have nearly identical statistical properties (such as mean, variance, and correlation), and gives rise to the same linear model when a regression routine is run on these datasets. However, the second dataset does not really constitute a linear relationship; a spline would fit the points better. The third dataset (at the bottom-left corner of figure 1.2) actually has a different regression line, but the outlier exerts enough influence to force the same regression line on the data. The fourth dataset is not even a linear relationship, but the outlier enforces the same regression line again.

These two examples demonstrate the importance of "seeing" our data before we blindly run algorithms and statistics. Fortunately, for visualization scientists like us, the world of data types is quite vast. Every now and then, this gives us the opportunity to create new visual tools other than the traditional graphs, plots, and histograms. These visual signatures and tools serve the same purpose that the graph plotting examples previously just did—spy and investigate data to infer valuable insights—but on different types of datasets other than just point clouds.

Another important use of visualization is to enable the data scientist to interactively explore the data. Two features make today's visualization tools very attractive—the ability to view data from different perspectives (viewing angles) and at different resolutions. These features facilitate the investigator in understanding both the micro- and macro-level behavior of their dataset.

Types of datasets

There are many different types of datasets that a visualization scientist encounters in their work. This book's aim is to prepare an enthusiastic beginner to delve into the world of data visualization. Certainly, we will not comprehensively cover each and every visualization technique out there. Our aim is to learn to use Mathematica as a tool to create interactive visualizations. To achieve that, we will focus on a general classification of datasets that will determine which Mathematica functions and programming constructs we should learn in order to visualize the broad class of data covered in this book.

Tables

The table is one of the most common data structures in Computer Science. You might have already encountered this in a computer science, database, or even statistics course, but for the sake of completeness, we will describe the ways in which one could use this structure to represent different kinds of data. Consider the following table as an example:

	Attribute 1	Attribute 2	...
Item 1			
Item 2			
Item 3			

When storing datasets in tables, each row in the table represents an instance of the dataset, and each column represents an attribute of that data point. For example, a set of two-dimensional Cartesian vectors can be represented as a table with two attributes, where each row represents a vector, and the attributes are the x and y coordinates relative to an origin. For three-dimensional vectors or more, we could just increase the number of attributes accordingly.

Tables can be used to store more advanced forms of scientific, time series, and graph data. We will cover some of these datasets over the course of this book, so it is a good idea for us to get introduced to them now. Although we will describe them in depth in the upcoming chapters, here we explain the general concepts.

Scalar fields

There are many kinds of scientific dataset out there. In order to aid their investigations, scientists have created their own data formats and mathematical tools to analyze the data. Engineers have also developed their own visualization language in order to convey ideas in their community. In this book, we will cover a few typical datasets that are widely used by scientists and engineers. We will eventually learn how to create molecular visualizations and biomedical dataset exploration tools when we feel comfortable manipulating these datasets.

In practice, multidimensional data (just like vectors in the previous example) is usually augmented with one or more characteristic variable values. As an example, let's think about how a physicist or an engineer would keep track of the temperature of a room. In order to tackle the problem, they would begin by measuring the geometry and the shape of the room, and put temperature sensors at certain places to measure the temperature. They will note the exact positions of those sensors relative to the room's coordinate system, and then, they will be all set to start measuring the temperature.

Thus, the temperature of a room can be represented, in a discrete sense, by using a set of points that represent the temperature sensor locations and the actual temperature at those points. We immediately notice that the data is multidimensional in nature (the location of a sensor can be considered as a vector), and each data point has a scalar value associated with it (temperature). Such a discrete representation of multidimensional data is quite widely used in the scientific community. It is called a scalar field. The following screenshot shows the representation of a scalar field in 2D and 3D:

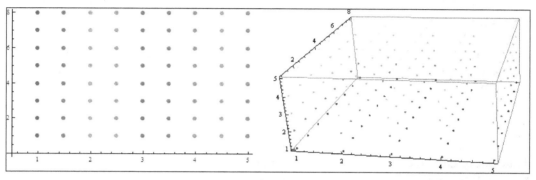

Figure 1.3 In practice, scalar fields are discrete and ordered

Figure 1.3 depicts how one would represent an ordered scalar field in 2D or 3D. Each point in the 2D field has a well-defined x and y location, and a single temperature value gets associated with it. To represent a 3D scalar field, we can think of it as a set of 2D scalar field slices placed at a regular interval along the third dimension. Each point in the 3D field is a point that has $\{x, y, z\}$ values, along with a temperature value.

A scalar field can be represented using a table. We will denote each $\{x, y\}$ point (for 2D) or $\{x, y, z\}$ point values (for 3D) as a row, but this time, an additional attribute for the scalar value will be created in the table. Thus, a row will have the attributes $\{x, y, z, T\}$, where T is the temperature associated with the point defined by the x, y, and z coordinates. This is the most common representation of scalar fields.

A widely used visualization technique to analyze scalar fields is to find out the isocontours or isosurfaces of interest. We will cover this in detail in *Chapter 3, Time Series and Scientific Visualization*. However, for now, let's take a look at the kind of application areas such analysis will enable one to pursue. Instead of temperature, one could think of associating regularly spaced points with any relevant scalar value to form problem-specific scalar fields. In an electrochemical simulation, it is important to keep track of the charge density in the simulation space. Thus, the chemist would create a scalar field with charge values at specific points.

For an aerospace engineer, it is quite important to understand how air pressure varies across airplane wings; they would keep track of the pressure by forming a scalar field of pressure values. Scalar field visualization is very important in many other significant areas, ranging from from biomedical analysis to particle physics. In this book, we will cover how to visualize this type of data using Mathematica.

Time series

Another widely used data type is the time series. A time series is a sequence of data points that are measured usually over a uniform interval of time. Time series arise in many fields, but in today's world, they are mostly known for their applications in Economics and Finance. Other than these, they are frequently used in statistics, weather prediction, signal processing, astronomy, and so on. It is not the purpose of this book to describe the theory and mathematics of time series data. However, we will cover some of Mathematica's excellent capabilities for visualizing time series, and in the course of this book, we will construct our own visualization tool to view time series data.

Time series can be easily represented using tables. Each row of the time series table will represent one point in the series, with one attribute denoting the time stamp—the time at which the data point was recorded, and the other attribute storing the actual data value. If the starting time and the time interval are known, then we can get rid of the time attribute and simply store the data value in each row. The actual timestamp of each value can be calculated using the initial time and time interval.

 Images and videos can be represented as tables too, with pixel-intensity values occupying each entry of the table. As we focus on visualization and not image processing, we will skip those types of data.

Graphs

Nowadays, graphs arise in all contexts of computer science and social science. This particular data structure provides a way to convert real-world problems into a set of entities and relationships. Once we have a graph, we can use a plethora of graph algorithms to find beautiful insights about the dataset. Technically, a graph can be stored as a table. However, Mathematica has its own graph data structure, so we will stick to its norm.

Sometimes, visualizing the graph structure reveals quite a lot of hidden information. As we will see in *Chapter 4, Statistical and Information Visualization*, graph visualization itself is a challenging problem, and is an active research area in computer science. A proper visualization layout, along with proper color maps and size distribution, can produce very useful outputs. In *Chapter 4, Statistical and Information Visualization*, we will demonstrate how to convert a dataset into a graph structure, how to create the graph in Mathematica, and how to visualize it with different layouts interactively.

Text

The most common form of data that we encounter everywhere is text. Mathematica does not provide any specific visualization package for state-of-the-art text visualization methods, but we will create a small and effective tool in *Chapter 4, Statistical and Information Visualization*, which shows the evolution and frequency of words in a document.

Cartographic data

As mentioned before, map visualization is one of the ancient forms of visualization known to us. Nowadays, with the advent of GPS, smartphones, and publicly available country-based data repositories, maps are providing an excellent way to contrast and compare different countries, cities, or even communities.

Cartographic data comes in various forms. A common form of a single data item is one that includes latitude, longitude, location name, and an attribute (usually numerical) that records a relevant quantity. However, instead of a latitude and longitude coordinate, we may be given a set of polygons that describe the geographical shape of the place. The attributable quantity may not be numerical, but rather something qualitative, like text. Thus, there is really no standard form that one can expect when dealing with cartographic data. Fortunately, Mathematica provides us with excellent data-mining and dissecting capabilities to build custom formats out of the data available to us. We will cover maps in *Chapter 5, Maps and Aesthetics*.

Mathematica as a tool for visualization

At this point, you might be wondering why Mathematica is suited for visualizing all the kinds of datasets that we have mentioned in the preceding examples. There are many excellent tools and packages out there to visualize data. Mathematica is quite different from other languages and packages because of the unique set of capabilities it presents to its user.

Mathematica has its own graphics language, with which graphics primitives can be interactively rendered inside the worksheet. This makes Mathematica's capability similar to many widely used visualization languages. Mathematica provides a plethora of functions to combine these primitives and make them interactive.

Speaking of interactivity, Mathematica provides a suite of functions to interactively display any of its process. Not only visualization, but any function or code evaluation can be interactively visualized. This is particularly helpful when managing and visualizing big datasets.

Mathematica provides many packages and functions to visualize the kinds of datasets we have mentioned so far. We will learn to use the built-in functions to visualize structured and unstructured data. These functions include point, line, and surface plots; histograms; standard statistical charts; and so on. Other than these, we will learn to use the advanced functions that will let us build our own visualization tools. Another interesting feature is the built-in datasets that this software provides to its users. This feature provides a nice playground for the user to experiment with different datasets and visualization functions.

From our discussion so far, we have learned that visualization tools are used to analyze very large datasets. While Mathematica is not really suited for dealing with petabytes or exabytes of data (and many other popularly used visualization tools are not suited for that either), often, one needs to build quick prototypes of such visualization tools using smaller sample datasets. Mathematica is very well suited to prototype such tools because of its efficient and fast data-handling capabilities, along with its loads of convenient functions and user-friendly interface. It also supports GPU and other high-performance computing platforms. Although it is not within the scope of this book, a user who knows how to harness the computing power of Mathematica can couple that knowledge with visualization techniques to build custom big data visualization solutions.

Another feature that Mathematica presents to a data scientist is the ability to keep the workflow within one worksheet. In practice, many data scientists tend to do their data analysis with one package, visualize their data with another, and export and present their findings using something else. Mathematica provides a complete suite of a core language, mathematical and statistical functions, a visualization platform, and versatile data import and export features inside a single worksheet. This helps the user focus on the data instead of irrelevant details.

By now, I hope you are convinced that Mathematica is worth learning for your data-visualization needs. If you still do not believe me, I hope I will be able to convince you again at the end of the book, when we will be done developing several visualization prototypes, each requiring only few lines of code!

Getting started with Mathematica

We will need to know a few basic Mathematica notebook essentials. Assuming you already have Mathematica installed on your computer, let's open a new notebook by navigating to **File | New | Notebook**, and do the following experiments.

Creating and selecting cells

In Mathematica, a chunk of code or any number of mathematical expressions can be written within a cell. Each cell in the notebook can be evaluated to see the output immediately below it. To start a new cell, simply start typing at the position of the blinking cursor. Each cell can be selected by clicking on the respective rightmost bracket. To select multiple cells, press *Ctrl* + right-mouse button in Windows or Linux (or *cmd* + right-mouse button on a Mac) on each of the cells. The following screenshot shows several cells selected together, along with the output from each cell:

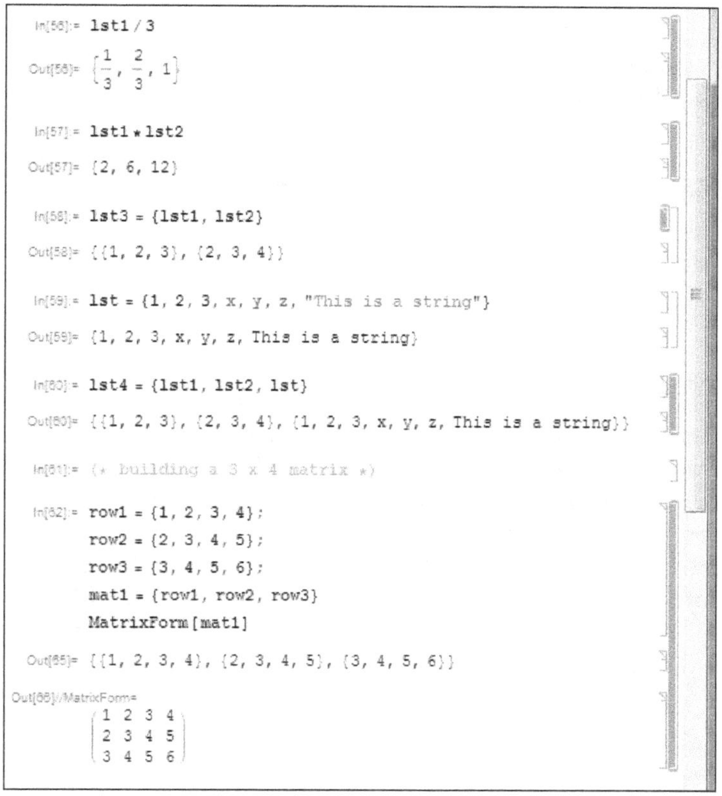

```
In[56]:= lst1 / 3

Out[56]= {1/3, 2/3, 1}

In[57]:= lst1 * lst2

Out[57]= {2, 6, 12}

In[58]:= lst3 = {lst1, lst2}

Out[58]= {{1, 2, 3}, {2, 3, 4}}

In[59]:= lst = {1, 2, 3, x, y, z, "This is a string"}

Out[59]= {1, 2, 3, x, y, z, This is a string}

In[60]:= lst4 = {lst1, lst2, lst}

Out[60]= {{1, 2, 3}, {2, 3, 4}, {1, 2, 3, x, y, z, This is a string}}

In[61]:= (* building a 3 x 4 matrix *)

In[62]:= row1 = {1, 2, 3, 4};
         row2 = {2, 3, 4, 5};
         row3 = {3, 4, 5, 6};
         mat1 = {row1, row2, row3}
         MatrixForm[mat1]

Out[65]= {{1, 2, 3, 4}, {2, 3, 4, 5}, {3, 4, 5, 6}}

Out[66]//MatrixForm=
         ( 1  2  3  4 )
         ( 2  3  4  5 )
         ( 3  4  5  6 )
```

Figure 1.4 Selecting and evaluating cells in Mathematica

We can place a new cell in between any set of cells in order to change the sequence of instruction execution. Use the mouse to place the cursor in between two cells, and start typing your commands to create a new cell. We can also cut, copy, and paste cells by selecting them and applying the usual shortcuts (for example, *Ctrl + C*, *Ctrl + X*, and *Ctrl + V* in Windows/Linux, or *cmd + C*, *cmd + X*, and *cmd + V* in Mac) or using the Edit menu bar. In order to delete cell(s), select the cell(s) and press the *Delete* key.

Evaluating a cell

A cell can be evaluated by pressing *Shift + Enter*. Multiple cells can be selected and evaluated in the same way. To evaluate the full notebook, press *Ctrl + A* (to select all the cells) and then press *Shift + Enter*. In this case, the cells will be evaluated one after the other in the sequence in which they appear in the notebook. To see examples of notebooks filled with commands, code, and mathematical expressions, you can open the notebooks supplied with this chapter, which are the polar coordinates fitting and Anscombe's quartet examples, and select each cell (or all of them) and evaluate them.

If we evaluate a cell that uses variables declared in a previous cell, and the previous cell was not already evaluated, then we may get errors. It is possible that Mathematica will treat the unevaluated variables as a symbolic expression; in that case, no error will be displayed, but the results will not be numeric anymore.

Suppressing output from a cell

If we don't wish to see the intermediate output as we load data or assign values to variables, we can add a semicolon (;) at the end of each line that we want to leave out from the output.

Cell formatting

Mathematica input cells treat everything inside them as mathematical and/ or symbolic expressions. By default, every new cell you create by typing at the horizontal cursor will be an input expression cell. However, you can convert the cell to other formats for convenient typesetting. In order to change the format of cell(s), select the cell(s) and navigate to **Format | Style** from the menu bar, and choose a text format style from the available options. You can add mathematical symbols to your text by selecting **Palettes | Basic Math Assistant**. Note that evaluating a text cell will have no effect/output.

Commenting

We can write any comment in a text cell as it will be ignored during the evaluation of our code. However, if we would like to write a comment inside an input cell, we use the (* operator to open a comment and the *) operator to close it, as shown in the following code snippet:

```
(* This is a comment *)
```

The shortcut *Ctrl + / (cmd + /* in Mac) is used to comment/uncomment a chunk of code too. This operation is also available in the menu bar.

Downloading the example code

You can download the example code files for all Packt books you have purchased from your account at http://www.packtpub.com. If you purchased this book elsewhere, you can visit http://www.packtpub.com/support and register to have the files e-mailed directly to you.

Aborting evaluation

We can abort the currently running evaluation of a cell by navigating to **Evaluation | Abort Evaluation** in the menu bar, or simply by pressing *Alt + .* (period). This is useful when you want to end a time-consuming process that you suddenly realize will not give you the correct results at the end of the evaluation, or end a process that might use up the available memory and shut down the Mathematica kernel.

Upcoming chapters

The next few chapters are divided according to the kinds of dataset we will tackle in each of them. *Chapter 2, Dissecting Data Using Mathematica*, will introduce us to data manipulation, cleaning, and fast-accessing techniques in Mathematica. We will also learn how to use some built-in plotting and styling functions in Mathematica. *Chapter 3, Time Series and Scientific Visualization*, will deal with scalar field visualization, along with some time-series visualization techniques. We will learn how to create a small molecular visualization tool and a time-series explorer. In *Chapter 4, Statistical and Information Visualization*, we will delve into the world of information visualization. While the types of information and their visualizations are quite varied in nature, we will focus on graph and text visualization in Mathematica. We will also learn some essential statistical visualization techniques.

This chapter will teach us how to build visualization tools such as the graph layout explorer, word frequency visualizer, and interactive chord charts. *Chapter 5, Maps and Aesthetics*, will focus on using cartographic data to build an interactive map visualization. We will end with a brief discussion on color maps and aesthetics in visualization. My suggestion would be to read each chapter without skipping any, because techniques introduced in each chapter will be used in subsequent chapters.

Further reading

The history of visualization deserves a separate book, as it is really fascinating how the field has matured over the centuries, and it is still growing very strongly. Michael Friendly, from York University, published a historical development paper that is freely available online, titled *Milestones in History of Data Visualization: A Case Study in Statistical Historiography*. This is an entertaining compilation of the history of visualization methods.

The book *The Visual Display of Quantitative Information* by *Edward R. Tufte* published by Graphics Press USA, is an excellent resource and a must-read for every data visualization practitioner. This is a classic book on the theory and practice of data graphics and visualization. Since we will not have the space to discuss the theory of visualization, the interested reader can consider reading this book for deeper insights.

Summary

In this chapter, we discussed the importance of data visualization in different contexts. We also introduced the types of dataset that will be visualized over the course of this book. The flexibility and power of Mathematica as a visualization package was discussed, and we will see the demonstration of these properties throughout the book with beautiful visualizations. Finally, we have taken the first step to writing code in Mathematica. Now we are ready to move onto the next chapter, where we will start writing some actual code to visualize data.

2
Dissecting Data Using Mathematica

We will go through a series of lessons in this chapter that will teach us the programming essentials to load, manipulate, and analyze different kinds of data. This will pave the way for the next few chapters on more advanced visualization techniques and tools. It is highly recommended that you try out and play with the code provided in the support section of the book's web page to understand the underlying concepts introduced in this chapter. Mathematica is a rich programming language that provides many functions to achieve miscellaneous tasks. We will only focus on the concepts and functions that are useful for our purpose. These lessons can be considered as a crash course on data manipulation and basic visualization using Mathematica, so buckle up and enjoy the ride!

Data structures and core languages

In the language of computer science, in order to handle any type of data, we need to load it in a convenient fashion in the memory. The constructs used to store data in the memory are called data structures. For most traditional programming languages, a programmer has to think and decide the right data structure to load and store the data, but Mathematica makes the work easy for us by providing a powerful core data structure that can be used in many different ways.

Lists are the fundamental and most useful data structure to load, manipulate, and store data in Mathematica. They provide a lot of flexibility for handling and representing different kinds of datasets. At the same time, they are simple enough that one can focus on the analysis instead of spending a lot of time coding or figuring out the right data structure to use.

Introducing lists

In order to create a new list and assign it to a list object, we simply use the expression {} (which means an empty list), or the command List[]. The following examples will create a list named lst:

```
lst = {}
```

or

```
lst = List[]
```

Each list can be treated as a mathematical object, and it can interact with constants and/or other list objects. A list may contain different data types as its elements, so it can be treated as a set or collection of objects. However, when the elements of a list are just numbers, it can then be treated as a tuple or an n-dimensional vector (where n is the number of elements in the list). The following code illustrates these points:

```
lst = {}
lst1 = {1,2,3}
lst2 = {2,3,4}
lst1 / 3
lst1 * lst2
lst={1,2,3,x,y,z,"This is a string"}
```

Here, we create an empty list lst by setting lst = {}. We really do not need to start by declaring every list empty; we might as well start with some elements in it. So we declare lst1 = {1, 2, 3} and lst2 = {2, 3, 4} to create two lists of length 3. Since lst1 and lst2 are now lists of numbers, evaluating lst1 / 3 or lst2 / 3 will divide each number in the list by 3. Moreover, we can do an element-wise multiplication between the two triplets (or three-dimensional vectors) simply by evaluating lst1 * lst2, which will return another list {2, 6, 12}. Finally, re-declare that lst with a mix of numbers (1, 2, and 3), symbols (x, y, and z), and a string. This type of mixing between different data types inside the same list is both allowed and perfectly plausible in Mathematica.

> A tuple is a representation of a set of numbers or objects. For example, {1, 2, 1} is a tuple of three elements. This can be used to represent a three-dimensional vector. In Mathematica, tuples are essentially lists that can be used to hold vectors of any dimension.

Nested lists

Lists may contain other lists. They are called list of lists, or simply a nested list. In order to demonstrate this concept, we can declare another list, lst3, as follows:

```
lst3 = {lst1,lst2}
```

Here, lst3 will then consist of {{1,2,3},{2,3,4}}. In this way, we can build even higher levels of nested lists. This provides a flexible way to build or store multidimensional datasets.

Matrices

We can use the concept of nested lists to build matrices. In order to build an *m* by *n* matrix of values (where *m* is the number of rows and *n* is the number of columns), we can treat each row of the matrix as a vector, or simply a list of length *n*, and we can have *m* such lists under a unified list, which will be our desired matrix. Let's enter the following code in our Mathematica notebook to create a *3* by *4* matrix:

```
(* building a 3 x 4 matrix *)
row1 = {1,2,3,4};
row2 = {2,3,4,5};
row3 = {3,4,5,6};
mat1 = {row1,row2,row3}
MatrixForm[mat1]
```

Note that we suppress the output of the first few lines by inserting a semicolon at the end of each line, and only outputting the final matrix, mat1, using a function MatrixForm (more on Mathematica functions later).Here, MatrixForm is a convenient function to display a list as a matrix. mat1 is a list of lists, where each sublist is a row of the matrix. The following figure 2.1 shows the list output and the matrix form after evaluating the cells:

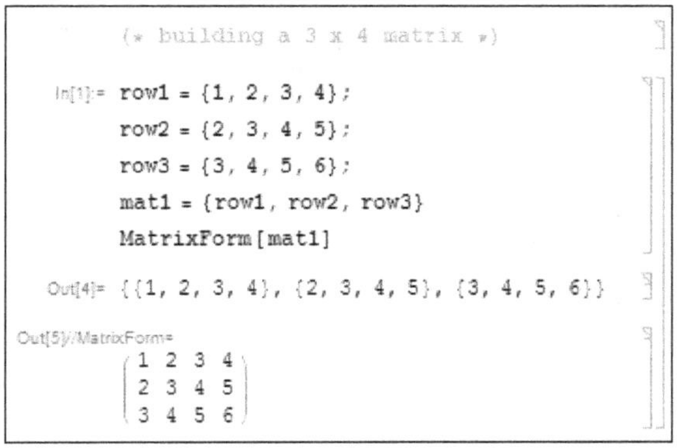

Figure 2.1 Creating matrices in Mathematica

Many datasets can be represented as matrices, and each entry of the matrix need not be a number in the case of different datasets. For example, a numerical dataset that contains text headers that provide the description of each column will have string elements in the first row.

Constructing lists programmatically

Often, we need to generate lists programmatically, or load our datasets into list structures by using a few commands. The preceding examples were used as a demonstration to explain the concept of lists in Mathematica. Now, we will take a deeper look at how lists can be constructed programmatically to build synthetic data, or load actual datasets into Mathematica. There are several functions that we can use to create lists of different kinds. From a generic data analysis and visualization perspective, the one that is mostly used is Table. It can be used to create vectors, arrays, matrix, and any other *n*-dimensional array.

Here is the basic syntax for calling the Table function:

```
Table[expr, {(i), (imin), imax, (di)}]
```

This syntax will return a list that contains the result of evaluation of the expression expr. expr may use i as an argument, where the iterator i takes on the values between imin and imax (inclusive), changing in steps of di. All arguments within the curly braces {..} are optional (and hence are put inside parentheses), except imax. If only imax is provided, the table will iterate from 1 to imax. To explain the syntax, let's take a simple expression that uses i, which is i itself:

```
Table[ i, {i, 1, 10, 2} ]
```

The code will generate a list shown as follows:

```
{1, 3, 5, 7, 9}
```

Here, i takes on values from 1 to 10, in steps of 2. Next, let's make the expression a little bit more interesting. We multiply a constant with i in expr in the following code snippet:

```
Table[ 10 * i, {i, 1, 10, 2} ]
```

The code will return the following list:

```
{10, 30, 50, 70, 90}
```

In fact, the function Table can be used to loop through different iterator variables. The following is a nested loop, which creates a nested list:

```
Table[ 10 * i + j, {i,1,10,2}, {j,1,10,4}]
```

The output will be as follows:

```
{{11,15,19},{31,35,39},{51,55,59},{71,75,79},{91,95,99}}
```

What is happening here? In our expression argument, we have 10 * i + j. The variable i iterates from 1 to 10 in steps of 2 (that is, {1, 3, 5, 7, 9}), and the inner iterator j iterates from 1 to 10 in steps of 4 (that is, {1, 5, 9}). i is our outer loop, and j is the inner loop. When we evaluate the expression 10 * i + j for each value of i, j iterates over the values 1, 5, and 9. For example, when i is 1, 10 * i + j will give the following result:

```
{10 * 1 + 1, 10 * 1 + 5, 10 * 1 + 9}
```

Each inner loop returns a list, thus {11, 15, 19} is the first list appended to the nested list. This continues for each value i takes on.

This nested list generation can be seen from the point of view of a matrix. Essentially, we have produced a 5 x 3 matrix, where the i loop goes through the rows, and the j loop goes through the columns. Each entry of the matrix is filled from the expression 10 * i + j.

Table entries with multiple elements

Table will evaluate any number of expressions given in the place of expr in the syntax for Table. This provides us with more control over the values of the entries in our array or matrix. Let's start off by giving a list as our expr. Use the following code snippet to create Table:

```
Table[
  {10 * i, 2 * j},
  {i,1,10,2},{j,1,10,4}
]
```

This produces a three-dimensional list:

```
{ {{10,2},{10,10},{10,18}}, {{30,2},{30,10},{30,18}},
{{50,2},{50,10},{50,18}}, {{70,2},{70,10},{70,18}},
{{90,2},{90,10},{90,18}} }
```

Figure 2.2 displays this as a matrix using the `MatrixForm[]` function as before:

```
In[6]:= Table[
         {10 * i, 2 * j},
         {i, 1, 10, 2}, {j, 1, 10, 4}
         ]
Out[6]= {{{10, 2}, {10, 10}, {10, 18}},
         {{30, 2}, {30, 10}, {30, 18}},
         {{50, 2}, {50, 10}, {50, 18}},
         {{70, 2}, {70, 10}, {70, 18}},
         {{90, 2}, {90, 10}, {90, 18}}}

MatrixForm[%]
```

$$
\begin{pmatrix}
\begin{pmatrix}10\\2\end{pmatrix} & \begin{pmatrix}10\\10\end{pmatrix} & \begin{pmatrix}10\\18\end{pmatrix} \\
\begin{pmatrix}30\\2\end{pmatrix} & \begin{pmatrix}30\\10\end{pmatrix} & \begin{pmatrix}30\\18\end{pmatrix} \\
\begin{pmatrix}50\\2\end{pmatrix} & \begin{pmatrix}50\\10\end{pmatrix} & \begin{pmatrix}50\\18\end{pmatrix} \\
\begin{pmatrix}70\\2\end{pmatrix} & \begin{pmatrix}70\\10\end{pmatrix} & \begin{pmatrix}70\\18\end{pmatrix} \\
\begin{pmatrix}90\\2\end{pmatrix} & \begin{pmatrix}90\\10\end{pmatrix} & \begin{pmatrix}90\\18\end{pmatrix}
\end{pmatrix}
$$

Figure 2.2 Using `MatrixForm` to visualize a matrix

Here, the `MatrixForm` function uses a `%` character as its argument. This merely asks the function to use the output in the last evaluation as its input argument.

In the expression for the `Table` function, we generate the two-element tuple `{10 * i, 2 * j}`, and each tuple is generated as one element in the 5 x 3 matrix. This is essentially the same as our previous example, but this time, we put a list (of length 2) in each entry instead of a single value.

In Mathematica, a line break does not affect the code as long as the brackets and parentheses match. In the previous piece of code, we have broken down the `Table` function into several lines. This is perfectly alright. When we type a function over several lines, Mathematica IDE automatically takes care of the tabs and spacing.

Let's look at how we can use multiple expressions inside the `Table` function. Often, it might be necessary to calculate some intermediate values that will be used by `expr`. We can simply use the semicolon character to suppress any intermediate calculation from getting into the final table:

```
Table[
    a = i+j;
    b = i*j;
    a + b,
    {i,1,10,2},{j,1,10,4}
]
```

The code produces the following nested list:

```
{{3,11,19}, {7,23,39}, {11,35,59}, {15,47,79}, {19,59,99}}
```

We again have a 5 x 3 matrix, but the elements in the matrix are the addition of a + b, where a and b are variables declared inside the `Table` function, and they take on the values i + j and i * j respectively as i and j change their values in each iteration.

We will learn more about Tables as we will be using the Table construct extensively in the book to create and combine different datasets. Mathematica provides many other useful functions to create lists, but the `Table` function is a generic and easy way to handle datasets, so we will mostly stick to it throughout the book. The `Table` function has a parallel version called `ParallelTable`, which can be used to do calculations in parallel. This is out of the scope of this book, but readers are encouraged to try it out once they are comfortable with the `Table` function.

Accessing elements from a list

There are many functions that Mathematica provides to access elements from a list. For data analysis and cleaning purposes, we will learn about the fastest and most elegant method to access a set of rows or columns from a matrix of values. The expression used to access the element of a list is [[ ]], where we define the desired range indices within the brackets. Let's look at the following few examples:

```
lst = Table[i*10,{i,50}] (* returns {10,20,30, .. ,480,490,500} *)
lst[[1]] (* returns 10 *)
lst[[10]] (* returns 100 *)
lst[[1;;10]] (* returns {10,20,30,40,50,60,70,80,90,100} *)
lst[[20;;30]] (* returns {200,210,220,..,280,290,300} *)
lst[[30;;]] (* returns {300,310,320,330,340,..,470,480,490,500} *)
lst[[;;]] (* gives the full list *)
```

At first, we create a list of numbers `1st`, which run from 10 to 500 in steps of 10, as {10, 20, 30, .., 500}, with a total of 50 elements in the list. Then, we access the elements of this list in different ways. Note that the index count starts from 1 in Mathematica, unlike in languages such as C or Java, where it starts from 0. `1st[[1]]` would return the first element in the list, which is 10. `1st[[10]]` would return 100, and so on. A powerful array access feature in Mathematica is demonstrated next. The double semicolon operator inside the array brackets [[ ]] represents a range. Writing the indices as `1;;10` is a shortcut to tell Mathematica that we want the elements ranging from the first index to the tenth index. Similarly, `1st[[20;;30]]` would return the 20th to the 30th elements (inclusive), as a list. When `;;` is used after an initial index number, it returns the rest of the list elements starting from that initial index (that is, `1st[[30;;]]` would return the 30th to 50th elements in the list). Providing the `;;` operator without any other index indicator will return the whole array.

 Throughout the book, we will use the words list, matrix, and array to denote the same data structure. In fact, we will only use a single Mathematica data structure (list) to work with matrices and arrays.

The `;;` operator works in the same way on any matrix of any dimensions. Next, we demonstrate the `;;` operator on a 2D matrix. We will use the following 6 x 6 matrix as our example:

2	3	4	5	6	7
4	6	8	10	12	14
6	9	12	15	18	21
8	12	16	20	24	28
10	15	20	25	30	35
12	18	24	30	36	42

Let's do the following operations on this matrix (or list of lists):

```
1st[[2,5]] (* returns 12 *)
1st[[1;;3]] (* returns {{2,3,4,5,6,7}
  ,{4,6,8,10,12,14},{6,9,12,15,18,21}} *)
1st[[1;;5,2]] (* returns {3,6,9,12,15} *)
1st[[1;;4, 2;;4]] (* returns {{3,4,5},{6,8,10}
  ,{9,12,15},{12,16,20}} *)
```

The matrix here is represented by a list that contains six sublists, each of which is a row of the matrix. Here, `lst[[2, 5]]` asks Mathematica to extract the second list's fifth element. The first index before the comma denotes which row we would like to access (in this case, the second row), and the second index defines the column number (in this case, the fifth column). Note that in the world of lists, we are merely asking Mathematica to return the second list's fifth element.

Next, we use the `;;` range operator to extract the first three rows. `lst[[1;;3]]` returns the first three sublists of `lst`. Then, to access the elements from the column of the matrix, we use the `;;` operator as `lst[[1;;5, 2]]`. This command asks Mathematica to parse through the rows 1 to 5, and extract elements from the second column. In order to extract the full column, we would use the following code snippet:

```
lst[[;;,2]]
```

Finally, we extract a submatrix from the matrix by parsing through some rows and some columns. `lst[[1;;4, 2;;4]]` goes through the rows 1 to 4 and the columns 2 to 4.

Applying set operations on lists

The [[ ]] operation is a shortcut for the command `Part`. There are several other useful set operations in Mathematica that we may need to learn in order to manipulate datasets. They are listed as follows with their syntaxes. We will eventually see some of them in action in the next few chapters:

- **Length**: This function simply returns the length of a list as a number. The syntax is as follows:

  ```
  Length[list]
  ```

  If the list is multidimensional, meaning it has sublists, then, to get the length of a sublist, we have to provide the sublist index too. For example, with a list like `lst = {{a,b,c}, {b,c,d,a}, {a,b}}`, if we want to get the length of the second sublist, we could use `Length[ lst[[2]] ]`, which will return 4.

- **Append**: The syntax for this is as follows:

  ```
  Append[list, elem]
  ```

  This returns a new list with the element `elem` appended to the end of `list`. A similar command is `AppendTo[list, elem]`, which appends `elem` at the end of `list` and resets `list` to the new list.

- **Flatten**: This is a very useful function that is used when we would like to flatten a list that contains many levels of sublists. This is often useful when we load data of some particular formats into one big list, and would want to redistribute the levels of each sublist.

  `Flatten[list]` would give us a new list with all levels flattened. For example, `Flatten[{a, b}, {c, {d}}]` would return {a, b, c, d}.

  `Flatten[list, n]` returns a list with only the *n*th level of lists being flattened. Thus, `Flatten[{a,b}, {c, {d}}, 1]` would collapse the first level only and will return {a, b, c, {d}}.

- **Union**: This is yet another very useful function that determines the union of a list. From the data manipulation perspective, this is quite useful for removing duplicates from a list.

  `Union[list1, list2, ...]` would return the union of the lists given as its argument. Note that the argument can be a single list too. The result is always sorted.

- **Partition**: This function is used to reshape an array or a matrix. There are several ways it takes its arguments. The commonly used form is as follows:

  `Partition[list, n]`, which divides a list into non-overlapping sublists that have length n. Thus, `Partition[{a, b, c, d, e, f}, 2]` will return {{a, b}, {c, d}, {e, f}}. Note that in this case, we reshaped a 1D array or a row of data into a matrix with three rows and two columns.

- **Tally**: This counts the number of times each element occurs in a list, and returns a new list that contains sublists of counts. The syntax is as follows:

  `Tally[list]`

  `Tally[{a,a,b,a,c,a,b,a}]` will return {{a, 5}, {b, 2}, {c, 1}}.

- **Select**: This function can be used to filter a list in many different ways. The syntax is as follows:

  `Select[list, crit]`

  Here, `crit` is a criterion expression that Mathematica applies on each element of the list. If the expression is evaluated as true, then the element passes. Otherwise, the element is discarded. For example, the following code snippet would return {2, 6, 12}:

  `Select[{1,2,6,12,13}, EvenQ]`

EvenQ is a Mathematica function that decides whether a number is even. In this case, EvenQ is applied to each element of the list, and the ones that are evaluated as true are returned. A more advanced example where we filter numbers that are greater than 3 is as follows:

```
Select[{1,2,3,4,5,-1,7}, # > 3 &]
```

This snippet will return {4, 5, 7}. We have two new expressions to learn from this example, so let's tackle them one by one. We can declare a function that takes each element of the list and tests whether the element is greater than 3. The expression # > 3 is a function expression that is applied to each element of the list. The # sign is used to denote the argument in this function expression. Each list element is treated as an argument passed to this function as Select goes through each of them. Now, we would like to declare the expression as a function. This is done by the & sign in Mathematica. It denotes that the expression is a pure function.

- **Position**: In order to find a certain element within a list, we can use this function. The syntax for this function is as follows:

```
Position[list, pattern]
```

This will search within the list and return the indices of the elements that match the pattern. For example, the following code snippet will return {{2}, {5}, {7}}:

```
Position[{a,b,a,a,b,c,b,c,d},b]
```

If we have lists of a higher dimension, the indices will be of a higher length. The following code snippet will return {{1,3}, {2,1}, {3,2}}:

```
Position[{{a,a,b},{b,a,a},{a,b,a}},b]
```

Here, we would like to search for b. b occurs in the first sublist at the third position. Thus, {1,3} is our desired index, and so on.

There are many other useful Mathematica functions that can be applied on lists. These functions will be used in the next few chapters, so refer to this list if you would like to review what each function does.

Functions and conditionals

Just like other programming languages, Mathematica lets us define our own functions. Other procedural programming constructs such as loops and conditionals are also there. However, it is better that we try to stick to the functional programming style instead of using For, Do, While, and other loops. This is mostly because some of these procedural programming constructs are known to be slow in Mathematica. It is almost always possible to use Table and similar functions to loop through and modify datasets. In this section, we will learn about writing our own functions and conditional expressions in Mathematica.

Declaring and using functions

For the purpose of data analysis and visualization, it is always useful to separate our code into different function calls. In this section, we will describe how to define our own custom functions in conjunction with variables and lists.

The basic function syntax is very simple. Here's an example of a simple function and its usage:

```
f[x_] := x^2
```

This function f takes a variable x and simply squares it. Each argument variable is declared by an underscore sign after it. x_ declares x as a variable inside the function. The colon followed by the equal operator := distinguishes between the function body code and the function name. Evaluating the function as f[2] will return 4. We can provide multiple arguments to a function in the same way, as shown here:

```
f[x_,y_] := Table[i^2+j,{i,1,x},{j,1,y}]
```

This function takes in two argument variables x and y, and uses them as bounds in a Table function. Note that this function returns a list. Evaluating f[2, 3] will return the list {{2,3,4}, {5,6,7}}.

If you are wondering whether Mathematica has a proper function declaration that has initialization, body, and return calls, similar to other popular languages like C or Java, here is an example of how to use these concepts in a Mathematica function:

```
scaleBySum[lst_,ind1_,ind2_] := Module[
{sum = 0, toReturn = {}},
sum = Total[ lst[[ ind1;;ind2 ]] ];
toReturn = lst[[ ind1;;ind2 ]] / sum;
Return[ toReturn ]
]
```

In this function, we take in a list and two numbers that are essentially start and end indices. Then, we divide the list elements that range from the start to end indices by the sum of the numbers within that range. There are several things going on here, but with Mathematica's syntax, we don't need to write a lot of code.

The function is called `scaleBySum`. It takes in the arguments `lst` (a list), `ind1` (the start index), and `ind2` (the end index). Next, we declare a `Module`, which is a nice way to structure our code. A `Module` has two sections. In the initialization section denoted within the curly braces, we initialize the variables that we will use within the function body. We initialize a variable called `sum` and set it to `0`. We also declare an empty list, `toReturn`, which will be populated with the results later. Next, we enter the function body, which is separated from the initialization section by a comma, and calculate the sum of the elements that range from the indices `ind1` to `ind2` using the function `Total`. `Total` is a built-in Mathematica function that returns the sum of a list. Next, we set `toReturn` to the sublist of interest that is divided by the sum. The built-in function `Return` returns the argument provided.

In practice, we will use the function as follows:

```
scaleBySum[{1,2,3,4,5},2,4]
```

This function will return the list $\{2/9, \ 1/3, \ 4/9\}$. The numbers 2, 3, and 4 are within the range defined by the index arguments, so they are divided by their sum, 9.

For now, this is all that we need to know about functions and using functions in our code.

Conditionals

In Mathematica, there are several conditional expressions that we can use. One that is commonly used is is the `If` condition. The syntax is as follows:

```
If[condition, texpr, fexpr, u]
```

If the `condition` evaluates to true, then `texpr` is evaluated. If `condition` evaluates to false, then `fexpr` is evaluated. If neither true nor false, then `u` is evaluated instead. Note that the fourth argument is optional. Here's an example of using the `If` conditional expression:

```
If[x > 0,
x = x/2; x++; x = x/3,
0]
```

The expression evaluates the condition to check whether x is greater than 0. If true, it executes the second line, which has a series of expressions that change x in certain ways. Intermediate outputs are suppressed by using semicolons. If x is not greater than 0, then the third line is executed instead. All of this could be written within one line; Mathematica does not really care about line breaks. However, it is advisable to break your code into different lines for clarity of reading.

Other conditional expressions are also there. If one does not want to write a series of If conditionals for a long list of conditional cases, the function Which can be useful. The syntax for the Which function is as follows:

```
Which[test1, value1, test2, value2, …]
```

Every test expression is followed by a series of expressions that is evaluated if the test expression is true. Take the following snippet as an example:

```
a = 1; Which[a == 1, x, a == 2, b]
```

This will return x.

Further core language

So far, what we have seen is a glimpse of what Mathematica's core programming language offers. These are the bare essentials you need to know if you are unfamiliar with Mathematica programming. For the purpose of data visualization coding, we will not need more than what is covered here. There are other utility functions that we will pick up along the way when necessary. If you would like to learn more on the Mathematica programming language, then you may look into the resources mentioned in the *Further Reading* section.

Data importing and basic plots

Equipped with a crash course on the Mathematica programming language, we can really start having some fun with data. The rest of the chapter will teach us how to load simple datasets and plot some values. We will learn about a few different kinds of plots and the methods of styling and customizing them.

Importing data into Mathematica

Mathematica provides a very rich data importing and exporting suite. The two commonly used functions to load data into a worksheet are Import and ReadList. In this section, we will use Import to load a dataset into Mathematica and plot it. We will style our plot, and explore some features of plotting functions that are useful.

SetDirectory[] and NotebookDirectory[]

To load our dataset, we need to tell Mathematica where to look for it. The structure of the code and data provided in the accompanying book's website follow the same pattern for every chapter. Under each chapter folder, there is a folder called data. The folder chapter2 contains our code notebooks for the preceding examples. We will start by setting the current path to our folder, as shown in the following code snippet:

```
SetDirectory[ NotebookDirectory[] ]
```

The SetDirectory function sets the current path to the file location string provided as its argument. The function NotebookDirectory[] returns the current notebook directory path as a string. Please note that we have to save our notebook at first for this to work.

Loading the dataset

The Import function takes in a file path string as its argument and returns the content of the file. Our dataset is a CSV (comma-separated values) time series file that has three columns. The column attributes are separated by commas. The first column holds the time values. The second and third columns represent two different time series that change over time. One is an exponential growth curve; the other is a sinusoidal function that exponentially amplifies over time. The interested reader may look into the DataGeneration.nb file (provided in the same folder) to see how the dataset is generated.

We load and organize the two time series using the following code.

```
dataset1 = Import["data/points_dataset1.csv"];
pointset1 = dataset1[[ ;;, 1;;2 ]];
pointset2 = dataset1[[ ;;, {1,3} ]];
```

The Import function looks under the data folder (we don't need to provide the full path, since we already set the file operation path to the current folder using SetDirectory) and loads the file named points_dataset1.csv. The file contents are stored inside the list dataset1. Here is a glimpse of the current content of dataset1:

```
{{0.,1.,0.},{0.2,1.04081,0.413554},{0.4,1.08329,0.843704},...}
```

Each row in the dataset contains three elements: time, y1, and y2, where y1 and y2 are two separate sets of data that evolve with time. Our next job is to put these two different series into two lists. The list for y1 should look like {{t1, y11}, {t2, y12}, {t3, y13}, ...}, where the subscripts denote the index of each row. We achieve this by declaring a new list called pointset1 and use our trusted friend, the part operator [[ ]], to extract data from all rows and include the first and second columns only. We do the same for the second series, but pick the first and third columns instead, and store the extracted list in pointset2. You can take out the semicolons at the end of each line and evaluate the cell(s) again to see the contents of each list at this point.

In the older Windows version of Mathematica, we may use two backslash characters (\\) as our file separator. In a Unix OS, this will be just a slash (/). The code provided with this book was written in Windows. However, if you have the latest version of Mathematica, you can simply use / as the file separator, regardless of the OS you are using.

Basic plotting functions

We have loaded the datasets; now it's time to visualize them. We will use the function ListPlot to plot the data and demonstrate some generic features applicable to many other plotting functions.

ListPlot

If we want to plot a single dataset that contains x and y values for 2D points, the syntax for ListPlot is as follows:

```
ListPlot[[{{x1,y1}, {x2,y2}, {x3,y3}, … }, options]
```

We have already put our dataset into this list form in the previous section, so we can go ahead and plot the datasets. The options are features embedded into the plot that we can change according to our needs. They are optional arguments. A few of these arguments are given as follows:

```
ListPlot[pointset1]
ListPlot[pointset2, AxesOrigin -> {0,0}, PlotRange -> All, Filling ->
Axis]
```

We can simply ask Mathematica to plot the data as points, or we could stylize our plot by adding some nifty features. `pointset1` is plotted with default arguments, and `pointset2` is plotted with several options. The following screenshot shows the plots:

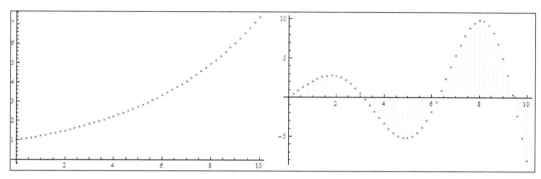

Figure 2.3 (left) `pointset1` with the default options, and (right) `pointset2` with the filling option enabled

The plot on the left is `pointset1`, and the plot on the right is from the list `pointset2`. With the default options, we get a point set representation on the axes. In order to customize the options, we will have to mention the name of the option argument, followed by the characters – and >, which represent the operator responsible for assigning some value to a property. We can add as many options as we want, each separated by a comma.

For the second plot, we have added the following options:

- `AxesOrigin`: This property is set to a pair of numbers that denote the origin of the graph in x and y coordinates. In the plot, we set them to (0, 0).

- `PlotRange`: This is used to define the plotting range. The value "All" asks Mathematica to stretch the graph to the maximum and minimum bounds of the graph. We could manually put a pair of numbers {*y*min, *y*max} instead of defining the vertical boundary.

- `Filling`: This property is used to fill the area within a defined region of the curve. We set a value to the x axis so that the area between the horizontal axis and the curve is filled.

Let's improve our plots further. The following points will help you add more features to your plots:

- We can also join the points in the plots. Mathematica interpolates between the points to create a smooth curve if we set the property `Joined` to `True`, as shown in the following code:

  ```
  ListPlot[pointset1,AxesOrigin->{0,0},PlotRange->All,Joined->True]
  ```

- The points and the joined curve can be made visible together using the `Mesh` property. Setting `Mesh` to `All` plots all the points too.

- We can combine the two plots into one plot. The `ListPlot` syntax for combining multiple plots is as follows:

  ```
  ListPlot[{list1, list2, …}, options]
  ```

  This way, we can plot both the lists within one figure.

- We can add a title to our plot by setting the `PlotLabel` option to the desired text.

- We can add axes labels to the plot using the `AxesLabel` option. It is set to a pair of strings that are the labels of the horizontal and vertical axes.

The code to accomplish these steps is as follows:

```
ListPlot[{pointset1,pointset2}, AxesOrigin->{0,0}, PlotRange->All,
Joined->True, Mesh->All, AxesLabel->{"time","y"}, PlotLabel->"y(t)"]
```

The following screenshot, figure 2.4, shows a plot (left) with the `Joined` property set to `True`, and the other part (right) shows the output from the given code:

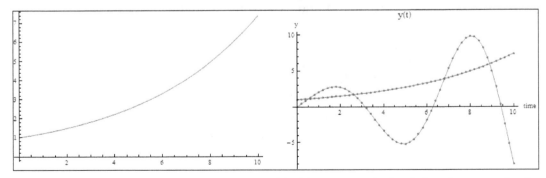

Figure 2.4 (left) The `Joined` option is set to `True`, and (right) points are joined and all meshes are rendered

Note that Mathematica automatically colors the lines differently. We can customize the line colors too, which will be discussed next.

Styling our plots

Let's experiment with more plotting features of Mathematica. Often, it is necessary to distinguish between curves when there are several plots combined into one plot. The Filling and PlotStyle features can be useful for this purpose.

We have seen how setting the Filling property to Axis fills the area between the curve and the axes. If we have several curves, it may be harder to distinguish them in this way. Mathematica automatically chooses different colors for filling as we increase the number of curves, but it may not be wise to use such a filling to begin with.

In the case of several curves on the same plot, we can leave them without specifying the filling property. Another interesting way is to fill the area between the curve intersections. This emphasizes the difference between the curves. To do this, we set Filling to {1->{2}}; this syntax asks Mathematica to fill the area from the first curve to the second curve, as shown in the following screenshot:

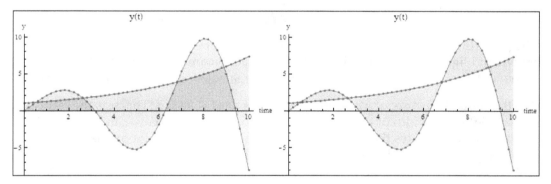

Figure 2.5 Different filling options: (left) fill to axis, and (right) fill between each other

The plot on the left shows how it would look if we filled the area towards the axis. Using our new Filling feature, we obtain the plot on the right, which emphasizes the difference between the curves.

We can change the color of our curves, and also the filling color, using PlotStyle and FillingStyle. Next, let's set the PlotStyle feature to a pair of colors (for two plots), and FillingStyle to another pair of colors:

```
ListPlot[{pointset1,pointset2}, AxesOrigin->{0,0}, PlotRange->All,
Joined->True, Mesh->All, AxesLabel->{"time","y"}, PlotLabel->"y(t)",
Filling->{1->{2}}, PlotStyle->{Brown,LightBrown}, FillingStyle-
>{Gray,LightGray}]
```

Mathematica has a set of predefined color names. We will be using these color names throughout the book. To see the list of colors, you can open the Color Palette from the Palettes menu on the menu bar. There are other ways to define a color, for example, using RGB values. We will demonstrate this shortly.

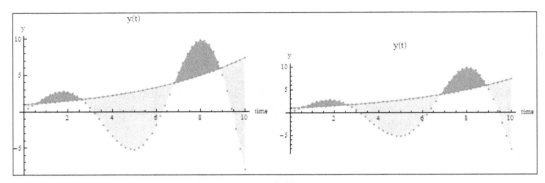

Figure 2.6 (left) More styling, and (right) aspect ratio

The preceding plots, figure 2.6, show the results. The curves are now colored brown and light brown respectively. The intersection area above the first curve (exponential growth) is colored gray, and the area below it is colored lighter gray.

Another notable feature of Mathematica plots is `AspectRatio`. This sets the ratio of the height and width of the plot. The default value is `Automatic`, in which case Mathematica calculates the ratio from the given datasets. The plot on the right is produced by changing the `AspectRatio` property to `0.4` (`AspectRatio->0.4`), and we can see that the plot height is squashed compared to the plot on the left.

The latest version of Mathematica, 10 as of this writing, allows us to style our plots with some quick themes and legends. In the suggestion bar that shows up below the latest output cell, there are options to set certain themes. The available themes range from `Classic` and `Web` to `Business` and `Marketing`. Instead of choosing these plot themes manually from the suggestion bar, we can insert the option `PlotTheme` inside our plotting functions to define these themes. For example, the following code will produce a plot that is automatically styled for presentation:

```
ListPlot[{pointset1,pointset2}, PlotTheme->"Marketing",
AxesOrigin->{0,0}, PlotRange->All, Joined->True, Mesh->All, AxesLabel-
>{"time","y"}, PlotLabel->"y(t)", Filling->{1->{2}}]
```

The following figure 2.7 shows the same plots displayed in figure 2.5, but with Marketing and Monochrome plot themes:

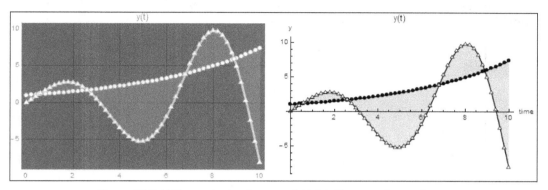

Figure 2.7 (left) The marketing theme, and (right) The monochrome theme

Plot legends

We can also include legends in our plots to distinguish between different datasets. The PlotLegends option allows us to insert different legends in our plots, depending on the type of plot. These are the following four types of legends available:

- LineLegend: This is used for function expression plots
- PointLegend: This is used for point list plots, as used in the examples of this chapter
- SwatchLegend: This is used for list plots, but with a different styling
- BarLegend: This is used for bar plots

The following code uses SwatchLegend to distinguish between the two list plots:

```
ListPlot[{pointset1,pointset2}, AxesOrigin->{0,0}, PlotRange->All,
Joined->True, Mesh->All, AxesLabel->{"time","y"}, PlotLabel->"y(t)",
Filling->{1->{2}}, PlotLegends -> SwatchLegend[{"data1","data2"}] ]
```

For our current datasets, we may also use the PointLegend feature. The following code incorporates the PointLegend feature and decorates the legend bar with a frame:

```
ListPlot[{pointset1,pointset2}, AxesOrigin->{0,0}, PlotRange->All,
Joined->True, Mesh->All, AxesLabel->{"time","y"}, PlotLabel->"y(t)",
Filling->{1->{2}}, PlotLegends-> PointLegend[Automatic,{"data1","da
ta2"}, LegendFunction->"Frame", LegendLabel->"datasets"] ]
```

Inside the `PointLegend` option, we have defined two additional legend functions. `LegendFunction` defines a styling option for the legend bar (a bounding frame in this case), and `LegendLabel` gives a title to the legend bar. The following figures 2.8 and 2.9 show the results of the preceding code:

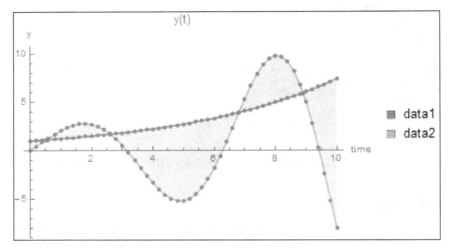

Figure 2.8 List plots with swatch legends

Note that the default styling in Mathematica 10 is slightly different from the versions 9 and 8; hence, the lines have different colors compared to the previous plots. The plots in this book are based on the classic styling option, so that Mathematica 8 and 9 users feel comfortable with the diagrams:

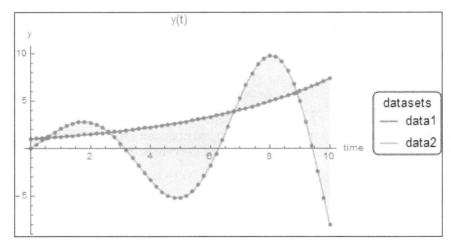

Figure 2.9 List plots with point legend and legend decoration

The accompanying notebooks and codes are carefully written so that they will work in all available versions (8, 9, and 10). However, a few functions and options in the book's code listings will not work in versions 8 and 9. They will be mentioned in the text clearly.

3D point plots

What if we want to see the evolution of both point sets in 3D? We have a time axis, and we have two series of data to go with it. This is the right time to demonstrate how we can plot a three-dimensional point cloud using a 3D scatter plot. The following syntax is similar to `ListPlot`:

```
ListPointPlot3D[{{x₁,y₁,z₁}, {x₂,y₂,z₂}, {x₃,y₃,z₃}, …}, options]
```

It takes in a list of {x, y, z} values. Remember that our original dataset list is in the correct format to be fed into this function. So, let's do that right away, as shown in the following code snippet:

```
ListPointPlot3D[dataset1, AxesLabel->{"time","y1","y2"}, PlotLabel-
>"y(t)", Filling->Bottom]
```

The plot on the left of figure 2.10 shows the output. We can see both the exponential growth and the sinusoidal behavior as time progresses. The `Filling` property allows us to track the exponential growth easily. In order to make it more apparent, we can color the points and the filling lines using the `ColorFunction` property. This is demonstrated in the plot on the right of the following screenshot:

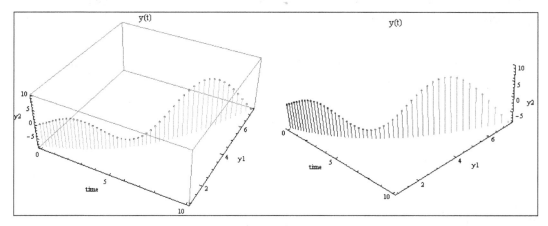

Figure 2.10 3D point plots with (left) axis filling, and (right) custom color function

The `ColorFunction` property is usually set to a function definition that takes in some values of the dataset and manipulates them to produce a color. To produce the preceding plot given in figure 2.10, let's write the following code:

```
ListPointPlot3D[dataset1, AxesLabel->{"time","y1","y2"}, PlotLabel-
>"y(t)", Filling->Bottom, Boxed->False, ColorFunction ->
Function[{x,y,z},RGBColor[x, y*0.5, 0]] ]
```

We declare the function using yet another Mathematica syntax. In this form of a function, the first argument is the list of variables used in the body. After the comma, the function definition follows. In this case, the function declares that the variables to be used are x, y, and z, which are placeholders for each row of data passed to this function. In the function definition, we produce a color value by using the `RGBColor` function. This has three arguments, which denote the values of red, green, and blue. Mathematica automatically scales the RGB values to stay between 0 and 1. Note that we left the third argument as 0, so the blue component is always absent in this custom color map.

We have also set the Boxed feature to `False`; this takes away the bounding box of the 3D plot.

Log plots

So far, we have been playing with nicely-behaving datasets. Let's get into some mess deliberately, because real world data is always messy. As a data visualization expert, you will often tackle datasets that have entries with very large values. Think about working with financial or economic data that have billions of dollars coexisting peacefully with only hundreds of dollars in the same dataset. Now, let's make the situation worse. Sometimes, we have data that can have unexpected big jumps in the values.

Figure 2.8 has a set of plots that show our effort to understand the large scale characteristics of a new dataset, shown as follows:

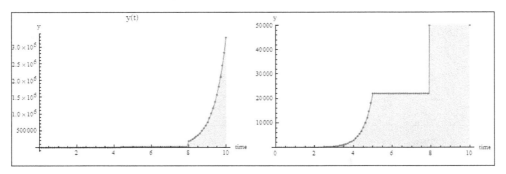

Figure 2.11 (left) Plotting on the normal scale, and (right) zooming on a shorter range of data

The following code was written in a new notebook to produce these plots:

```
SetDirectory[NotebookDirectory[]]
logdata = Import["data\\points_dataset2.csv"];
ListPlot[logdata, AxesOrigin->{0,0}, PlotRange->All, Joined->True,
Mesh->All, AxesLabel->{"time","y"}, PlotLabel->"y(t)", Filling->Axis]
ListPlot[logdata, AxesOrigin->{0,0}, Joined->True, Mesh->All,
AxesLabel->{"time","y"}, PlotLabel->"y(t)", Filling->Axis,
PlotRange->{0,50000}]
```

The dataset is loaded in a similar manner using the `Import` function. Using `ListPlot`, we plot the data to initiate our investigation. Since the values on the vertical axis are quite large, we change the `PlotRange` option to focus on a smaller range of values in the next plot. Now, the range is set between 0 and 50,000. The bigger values swamped the initial nature of the curves, as we can see that the initial plot shows a flattened curve in the beginning. However, there really is an exponential growth.

We can keep playing around with the plotting range to discover features like this, or we can use log plots. Log plots are often used to observe the characteristic changes in the larger range without collapsing the features of the smaller range of the graph. In case of an exponential growth (for example, bacterial culture growth or investment with interest), a vertical logarithmic scale will reveal constant growth rates (if present), which is often useful for predicting long-term behavior.

In the following code the functions `ListLogPlot` and `ListLogLogPlot` have the same syntax as `ListPlot`, but change the axes to log scale. `ListLogPlot` has a vertical log scale, and `ListLogLogPlot` has both a vertical and horizontal log scale:

```
ListLogPlot[logdata, AxesOrigin->{0,0}, PlotRange->All, Joined->True,
Mesh->All, AxesLabel->{"time","y"}, PlotLabel->"y(t)", Filling->Axis]
ListLogLogPlot[logdata, PlotRange->All, Joined->True, Mesh->None,
AxesLabel->{"time","y"}, PlotLabel->"y(t)", Filling->Axis]
```

The output of this code is shown in the following screenshot:

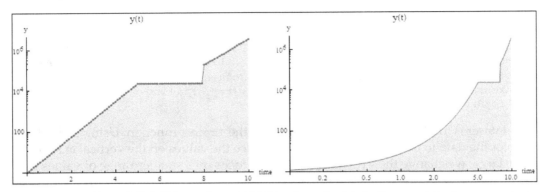

Figure 2.12 (left) Log scale, and (right) log-log scale plots for the same dataset

In the case of a vertical log scale, we discover features in the dataset that could not be seen with `ListPlot`. There are two exponential growth regions in the data. We possibly have a straight line with a positive slope between $t = 5.0$ and $t = 8.0$, and then there is a large jump in value at around $t = 8.0$. The log-log plot somewhat retains the macro-level shapes of the piecewise curves.

Further reading

The Mathematica Journal is a free journal with a wonderful community where experts and intermediate users share their thoughts and tips on programming with Mathematica. Interested readers can access the current and previous volumes in the following link: `http://www.mathematica-journal.com/`.

Mathematica has loads of functions that are used to manipulate lists. The same goes for the amazing number of options it offers to customize our plots. We will cover some more plots in the upcoming chapters, but we cannot possibly list every feature and function. Our goal is to learn visualization by developing some small projects. An introductory book that introduces Mathematica programming to beginners is *Programming with Mathematica* by Paul Wellin. The Mathematica documentation is a very good resource to find all the plotting options and their usage. Other useful list-manipulation techniques are also described in several tutorials in the documentation. When in doubt, or if you simply cannot remember a function or a feature, press *F1*!

Summary

In this chapter, we have learned the basics of Mathematica programming that are essential for data loading and manipulation. Some frequently used list operations are described, along with the basics of functions and conditionals. We encounter numerical datasets for the first time in the book, using `Import` to load the datasets into Mathematica. The datasets are visualized using the `ListPlot`, `ListPointPlot3D`, and `ListLogPlot` commands. We have also learned about some basic styling of our plots. In the next chapter, we will look at more ways to visualize time series data, and get a taste of visualizing some commonly used scientific data formats.

3
Time Series and Scientific Visualization

We finished the last chapter with some basic plots to explore time series data. Time series visualization is an important tool that is used in many fields, including finance, economics, digital signal processing, and so on. Understanding how asset values evolve over time is an integral part of modeling and predicting fluctuations. Visualizing the wave properties of electrical signals over time helps us understand the underlying physics. Regardless of what signal we choose to analyze, seeing its micro and macro behavior at different resolutions over different durations reveals valuable information about it.

Any time series can be essentially interpreted and/or modeled as a signal. A quantitative analyst in Wall Street treats a series of daily stock price data as a stochastic signal with certain mathematical properties that can be measured and calculated from the signal. In the realm of mathematics, any time series data interpreted as signals can be given some meaning in this way, which can be someone's daily activity, monthly electricity usage, a country's GDP over decades, and so on. Visualization plays an important part in seeing trends in time series, and it also helps in deciding what kind of mathematical tools can be applied to the dataset.

Time series visualization overlaps with scientific visualization. Scientific data comes in many forms. Time series is one of the most widely used data types. Among other types of dataset, scalar fields (as discussed in *Chapter 1*, *Visualization as a Tool to Understand Data*) are commonly used by scientists and engineers to understand the characteristics of a quantity measured in a well-defined volume of space. In this chapter, we will learn some more visualization techniques for time series data, along with the methods to visualize scalar field data.

The emphasis will be on mastering Mathematica's interactive graphics programming language to visualize some real-world data. Mathematica provides many plotting functions to plot different forms of time series and scalar field datasets. Instead of listing all of the function names with examples, we will dig a little deeper and explore how we can create custom visualization tools to solve different scenarios.

Periodic patterns in time series

Often, there are recurring trends in the data that suggest a periodic pattern, and simple plotting of the time series (like what we did in *Chapter 2, Dissecting Data Using Mathematica*) might not reveal such patterns. Besides, some datasets are inherently periodic. The daily Internet usage of a community can be represented as the hourly percentage of people using the Internet over a span of 24 hours. We can collect such data for a month and visualize any visible trend present in the data. So, what we will have is a percentage number between 0 and 1, recorded for each hour over 30 days. If we are given such a structured dataset, it might not be wise to simply plot the points over time. We would like to compare hourly activity side by side so that we can compare any difference on an hourly basis.

There is an easy solution if we want to stick to point plotting. We can use the `Table` function and the `;;` operator to divide the data into 30 sets of equal length; this way we will divide the dataset into daily Internet activities. We can also use the `Partition` function (introduced in *Chapter 2, Dissecting Data Using Mathematica*) to achieve this. Some of these datasets can be graphed in the same plot to compare the hourly values. This is all good, except if we want to compare several days and the plots start to get cluttered with many lines. If the percentage values are nearer to one another, it will be hard to compare the different values at the same hour.

In such cases, a common practice among visualization scientists is to use a visual representation that is inherently periodic. This is the whole idea behind spiral charts and sector charts. Before we move on to how we can create a sector chart using Mathematica, let's take a look at some examples. The example data for the charts are simulated by the author using a simple observation—we tend to use the Internet in the weekend evenings more than in the weekend mornings. On the other hand, due to office activities, we expect more people to use the Internet during the daytime, with a peak around the afternoon hours.

The following figure shows two sector charts, where an angular section represents a duration of one hour, and the radial length of the bar in each of the sections represents the percentage Internet activity for that hour. Therefore, each ring represents a day (with 24-hour ticks), and we essentially have a radial bar chart for every day, where hourly activities can be compared very easily over a number of days. One figure shows the activity for two weekdays, and the other shows a weekday going onto a weekend day. Can you guess which one is which?

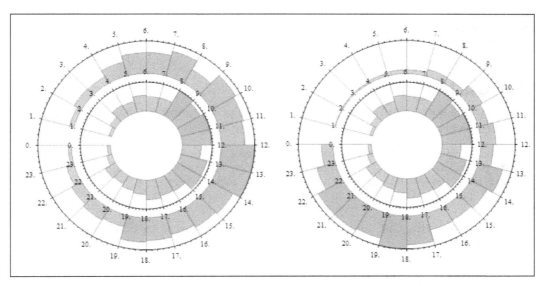

Figure 3.1 Two sector charts showing daily Internet usage, each for a period of two days

The chart on the left shows that both days (that is, both rings) have a peak activity at around noon, so we conclude that this represents the two weekdays. The chart on the right has the inner ring peaking at around noon; the outer ring has a peak during the evening time. So, we conclude (based on our simple model) that the figure on the right shows one weekday and a weekend day.

Sector charts

Sector charts can easily be created using Mathematica as it provides a built-in function to do so. The syntax is:

```
SectorChart[data, options]
```

Here, `data` needs to be in the form $\{\{x_1, y_1\}, \{x_2, y_2\}, \ldots\}$. Here, x_i represents the sector angle of a particular bar, and y_i represents the radial length of the bar. Mathematica will scale the values appropriately to take account of the maximum and minimum values present in the dataset. If we want to plot several charts together (like in the previous figure, where we visualized two different datasets representing the activity over two days), the syntax is simple enough:

```
SectorChart[{data1, data2, …}, options]
```

Here, each of the datasets needs to have the same structure as the preceding code snippet.

Simulating Internet activity

Let's generate some simulated Internet activities of a community based on our simple weekday-weekend activity model. The following code models the Internet usage:

```
(* a simple weight function that models internet usage over 24 hours
in a working day. The community reaches the peak of usage in the noon,
and most go to sleep at 12 am, except the coders! *)
wf = Table[ Sin[x], {x, 0, Pi, Pi/24.0} ] [[1;;24]];

(* a model for the weekend, when people use more internet in the
evening *)
wf2 = Table[ Sin[x] * Exp[x], {x, 0, Pi, Pi/24.0} ] [[1;;24]];
wf2 = wf2 / Max[wf2];
```

Before we explain this piece of code, let's look at the graphs of `wf` and `wf2` in the following figure:

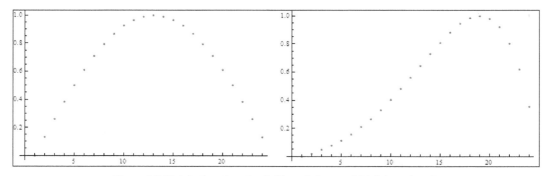

Figure 3.2 Weight functions for (left) weekdays and (right) weekends

Here, we declare two weight arrays. Each has 24 elements. The `wf` array (on the left) is sampled from a sinusoidal function over 0 to Pi, so we have the upper half of a sine curve and get a peak value at the middle of the curve. The values are between 0 and 1. This represents a weekday's hourly activity. The `wf2` array is sampled in the same way, but this time the function is chosen in such a way that the activity rises as we reach 9 and 10 p.m., and falls off quickly as we go to sleep by 12 a.m. (assuming no one goes to late-night hangouts and parties). Each value is scaled to lie within 0 and 1 by dividing it with the maximum value present in the set.

You might be wondering why we are calling these weight arrays. This is because of what we are going to do next. If we simply take these values as the percentage of active people, then there is no random element involved here. Next, we will choose a set of random numbers (between 0.5 and 1) for each hour, and multiply each set of daily activity model (`wf` or `wf2`) with these numbers, to get a randomly distributed hourly activity set that roughly follows our model:

```
(* simulate two weekdays with some randomness *)
data1 = Partition[
 Riffle[ ConstantArray[1,24], RandomReal[{0.5,1}, 24] * wf ]
 , 2 ];
data2 = Partition[
 Riffle[ ConstantArray[1,24], RandomReal[{0.5,1}, 24] * wf ]
 , 2 ];

(* simulate a weekend *)
data3 = Partition[
 Riffle[ ConstantArray[1,24], RandomReal[{0.5,1}, 24 ] * wf2 ]
 , 2];
data4 = Partition[
 Riffle[ ConstantArray[1,24], RandomReal[{0.5,1}, 24 ] * wf2 ]
 , 2];
```

There are several function calls here to prepare our dataset in the format required by the `SectorChart` function. Let's deconstruct the code for one dataset from the bottom of the function calls. We create an array of random values using the `RandomReal` function. The function syntax in our case looks like `RandomReal[{min, max}, num]`, which returns a list of length `num` containing uniformly distributed values drawn from the range defined by `min` and `max`. This randomly generated array is multiplied with `wf` or `wf2` to create our desired 24-hour activity list.

The `SectorChart` function requires a dataset in the format $\{\{x_1, y_1\}, \{x_2, y_2\}, ...\}$. In our case, since we are looking at the hourly activity, all the x_i values will be 1. So, we next create an array of ones with the `ConstantArray` function. `ConstantArray[value, num]` returns an array of length `num`, with the array elements filled with `value`.

Now we have two lists that have our x_i and y_i values. The `Riffle` function takes in two lists, and returns a combined list where the elements are taken from each array in an alternating fashion. For example, `Riffle[{a, b, c}, {d, e, f}]` will return the list `{a, d, b, e, c, f}`. Using `Riffle` with our x and y lists, we now have a list of the form $\{x_1, y_1, x_2, y_2, ...\}$. Finally, we use `Partition` to divide this list into a set of non-overlapping sublists, each of length 2. This gives us our desired $\{\{x_1, y_1\}, \{x_2, y_2\}, ...\}$ format.

SectorChart and its options

The same code structure is used to generate four datasets. Let's visualize some of the datasets using the `SectorChart` command with no options:

```
SectorChart[data1]
SectorChart[{data1,data2}]
```

The following figure (left: `data1` and right: `data1` and `data2` combined) shows the sector charts:

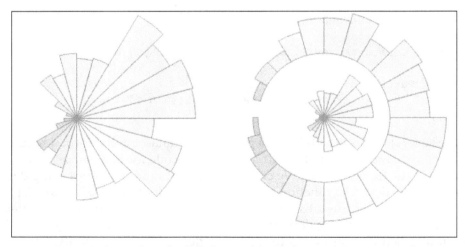

Figure 3.3 Sector charts for (left) data1 and (right) data1 and data2 combined

The default `SectorChart` options color the bars according to the angular distance covered, so the bars are colored as the day progresses. However, since we are more interested in the hourly difference between the days, we will like our color map to color the bars according to the height of the bars. Also, note that the inner ring starts from the origin (0, 0). For visual consistency with the other outer rings, we will make the origin start at (0, 1) in polar coordinates. Most importantly, we do not have grids and labels on the chart, so let's stylize our charts using the following code:

```
(* draw the sector chart of internet usage in the working days *)
SectorChart[ {data1,data2}, SectorOrigin->{Automatic,1}, PolarAxes-
>{True, False}, PolarGridLines->{Automatic,None}, PolarTicks-
>{Automatic,None}, ColorFunction-> Function[ {x,y}, Hue[x, y*0.5, 0.5,
0.5] ]
]
```

The options are listed in the following points:

- `SectorOrigin`: This decides where to start the polar coordinate origin of the sector chart. The {`Automatic`, `1`} parameters tells it to find the optimal angular coordinate and set the radial coordinate to 1. It leaves an empty circular space in the origin.

- `PolarAxes`: This determines whether to display axes in the angular and radial directions. We choose to have only the hour ticks, so we set angular ticks to `True` and radial ticks to `False`.

- `PolarGridLines`: This determines whether to display grids in the angular and radial directions. We will like to emphasize each hour so that we can compare between the hourly activities seamlessly. The angular grids (representing the hours) are set to `Automatic` and radial grids are set to `none` to reduce the clutter in the visual information.

- `PolarTicks`: This determines what labels to put as the tick values along the axes. We label each hour by setting the angular component to `Automatic`, and the radial component to `none`.

Finally, we create a custom color map to suit our needs. Similar to the plot in *Chapter 2, Dissecting Data Using Mathematica*, we define our own `ColorFunction` by a function that takes in a pair of values, {x, y}, as its argument. Each pair of values in the dataset is passed to this function, and it calculates a color value using the `Hue` function. The `Hue` function represents a color in the **HSB (Hue, Saturation, and Brightness)** color space, which is a different color space compared to our known RGB colors. It takes in three values for the H, S, and B components, and another additional value that determines the opacity of the bars. We create semi-transparent bars by providing an opacity value of 0.5.

Let's look at the result of changing these options in the following screenshot:

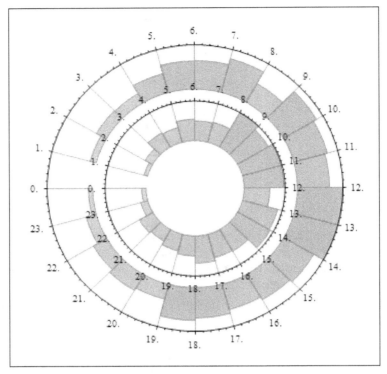

Figure 3.4 Styled sector chart

We now have grids, hour ticks, an appropriate color map (based on the radial height, not angular distance), and a proper sector origin. This makes it quite easy to track the changes along a particular hour across several days.

The figure becomes a little bit cluttered if we try to visualize all the days together. You can try and plot the four datasets to see how they look. The grid lines guide us to distinguish between hours; however, an experienced user of this chart might not need any guidance to see the global trends. Next, we plot all 4 days of data in the same plot, and take out the grids just so the global trends are emphasized, using the following code:

```
(* move from weekdays to weekends *)
SectorChart[ {data1,data2,data3,data4}, SectorOrigin->{Automatic,1},
PolarAxes->{True,False}, PolarGridLines->{True,None}, PolarTicks-
>{None,None}, ColorFunction-> Function[ {x,y}, Hue[x, y*0.5, 0.5, 0.5]
]
]
```

The result is demonstrated as follows:

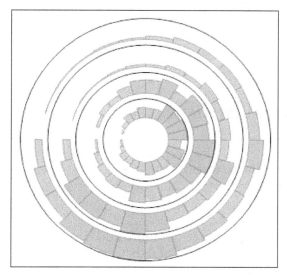

Figure 3.5 Visualizing several days' activity together

The trends and peaks are clearly visible in this visualization, and adding some more days will still maintain the simplicity, revealing the general trends over days.

Note that we can use SectorChart in other scenarios where both the angular and radial component vary. For the purpose of periodic time series visualization, we should stick to the repetitive component (angular direction) as time and set the observed value at each time point as the radial component.

The SectorChart function has a 3D version, called SectorChart3D, with the additional dimension of height. This can be useful to monitor another dimension of data associated with the time series.

Interactive visualization of financial data

Financial time series data is random in nature, and any visible patterns in such data depend on many market factors. From the perspective of visualization, it is best to build customized tools to monitor the variables of interest, instead of using the general plotting tools that are available to us. Mathematica provides a set of financial data-plotting tools that are suitable for quantitative analysts and market researchers. These tools require specific knowledge of advanced financial analysis. Instead of covering these in detail, we will focus on solving data visualization case studies according to our needs.

Keeping up with the spirit of the book, which is to learn how to create custom visualization tools in different scenarios, we will now build an interactive visualization tool to monitor a financial time series at different resolutions interactively. The code can be changed very easily to calculate and monitor different variables of interest over time. In the process, we will start to get deeper into the graphics programming language that Mathematica provides to its programmers.

The DateListPlot function

A common form of financial time series that we encounter is as a date stamp with the stock price for that day. Mathematica has a rich collection of example datasets that include some financial time series data too. Let's start by loading the stock price values for IBM, using the following code:

```
data = FinancialData["IBM", All];
```

The `FinancialData` function is a custom function that takes in an entity name as its first argument and returns a range of data from the pool of data available for that particular entity. In this case, we loaded the stock price values of IBM, and we asked Mathematica to provide us the full range of data in the second argument. The data format is { {{2011, 9, 20}, 166.97}, {{2011, 9, 21}, 165.34}, ... }, where every element in the list contains a date list in the {year, month, day} format, followed by the stock price value. We can use the `DateListPlot` function to visualize this data, as shown in the following code snippet:

```
DateListPlot[data, Joined->True, Filling->Bottom]
```

The output of this code snippet is shown in the following screenshot:

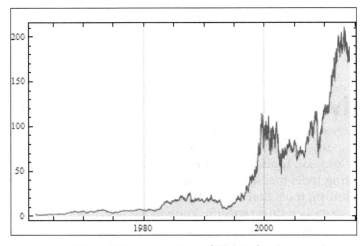

Figure 3.6 `DateListPlot` of IBM stock prices

The `DateListPlot` function is a special variant of `ListPlot` that shares the same syntax and many options. As we can see, the available data range is from around 1960 to 2014. We can also see the global trend from this plot. What is not present is a custom zoom tool that lets us dynamically select a data range and see the fluctuations and actual data points, which we will build. The following screenshot shows what the end product will look like:

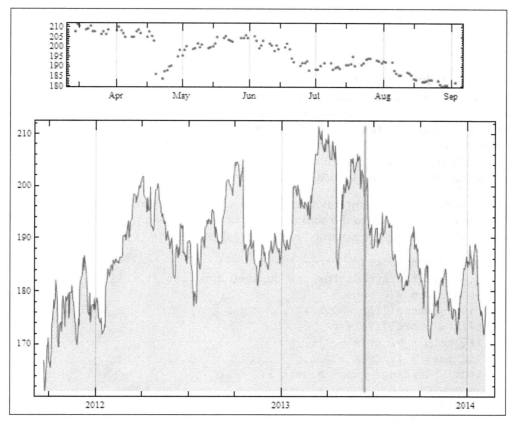

Figure 3.7 `DateListPlot` interactive zooming tool

We have two plots in this visualization. The bottom plot shows the overall dataset, and the top plot works as an inset; moving the mouse pointer over the bottom plot will move the vertical gray line horizontally along with the pointer, and the inset window will show a range of dates and the raw values of the stock price (without interpolation) around that line, centering the inset plot at the position of the gray line.

Adding interactivity – preliminaries

We will work with a much smaller range of data to demonstrate our code. To be precise, let's work with the latest 600 records. Let's calculate some other essential quantities too. This is achieved by using the following lines of code:

```
data = data[[-600;;]];
yearmin = Min[ data[[;;,1,1]] ]
yearmax = Max[ data[[;;,1,1]] ]
datamin = Min[ data[[;;,2]] ]
datamax = Max[ data[[;;,2]] ]
```

With the negative indexing, we ask Mathematica to set the data to the last 600 records. Then, we calculate the minimum and maximum years present in this reduced dataset. The `data[[;;, 1, 1]]` function provides a list of years (selecting all records, choosing the first element that is a date, and then getting the first element of the date, which is the year number). Here, `Min` and `Max` give the minimum and maximum values in this list. Next, we calculate the minimum and maximum stock price values similarly.

We then write the following function that will convert a pair of coordinate values on the plot image to the actual dataset range indices it will represent. The coordinate values are assumed to be normalized to a [0, 1] scale:

```
mapCoordToInd[coord_, range_]:=
 (* =!= is the symbol for the UnsameQ function *)
 Which[coord =!= None,
  tmin = coord[[1]] - 0.1;
  tmax = coord[[1]] + 0.1;
  If[ tmin < 0, tmin = 0];
  If[ tmax > 1, tmax = 1];
  ind1 = Ceiling[ range * tmin ];
  ind2 = Ceiling[ range * tmax ];
  If[ ind1 < 1, ind1 = 1];
  {ind1, ind2}
  ,
  coord == None,
  ind1 = 1;
  ind2 = range;
  {ind1, ind2}
 ]
```

The function takes in `coord`, which is a pair of coordinate values, and the length of the dataset list as the `range` variable. Using a `Which` conditional statement, we decide whether the value of `coord` is not `None` (the `=!=` operator is similar to the *not equals* operator). If this is so, we calculate `tmin` and `tmax` to get a range centering the `coord` value. Then, we constrain `tmin` and `tmax` so that they do not go beyond the [0, 1] range. Next, `range` is multiplied with `tmin` and `tmax` to get the desired lower and upper indices that we will use to extract a smaller range of data from the actual dataset. We return these indices as a pair. If the value of `coord` is `None`, which is the case when the mouse pointer is not on top of the main plot, we simply set the indices to include the full range of data.

We write the function in a separate cell and evaluate the cell to compile the function. This function will be called every time there is a mouse movement over the main plot. We will extract the normalized mouse coordinate position within the plot image using the `MousePosition` function, and pass it on to the above function to get back a range of index values, in order to plot a reduced dataset. The `MousePosition` function will need to be updated dynamically, which is where the actual interactivity functions of Mathematica enter the scene. Before we talk about dynamic interactivity, let's pause for a while to familiarize ourselves with the graphics package of Mathematica.

Intermission – Graphics and Show

We will use the graphics package quite a lot throughout the rest of the book to create visualizations. Graphics is a powerful package to draw graphic primitives in a canvas. Starting from circles, lines, and rectangles, we can render text and other shapes on the canvas. We can combine different graphic elements and canvases to create custom plots and visualization. Every plot we create in Mathematica is a graphics element, so they can be combined with other primitive shapes too.

The graphics package is quite simple to use. Let's start by creating a circle, using the following line of code:

```
Graphics[ Circle[ ] ]
```

This code will create a canvas with a circle of unit radius. The real syntax of graphics is as follows:

```
Graphics[{properties1, element1, properties2, element2, …}]
```

Each drawing element's property needs to be described before we issue the command to draw the element. The property arguments are optional, or can be more than one, as demonstrated in the following code:

```
g1 = Graphics[{ Thick, Black, Circle[{0,0}], Thin, Blue,
Circle[{3,3}], Gray, Text["Example Text",{2,2}] }]
```

This creates a canvas with a circle centered at (0, 0), another circle centered at (3, 3), and a text starting at the coordinates (2, 2). By default, the circle has a radius of 1, unless we ask Mathematica to use a specific radius. Study the following figure 3.8 to see what the canvas looks like.

Let's create another line, and combine the two different graphic elements into one canvas:

```
g2 = Graphics[{ Thick, Black, Dashed, Line[{{0,3}, {3,0}}] }]
Show[g1, g2]
```

Here, we create a thick and dashed line using the `Line` function, which takes in a set of points to draw lines between them. In this case, the line is rendered from (0, 3) to (3, 0). We store this graphic element in a variable named g2, and we show g1 and g2 together using the `Show` command. This command is used to combine a variety of graphic elements. In the following screenshot, the left half of the image shows g1, while the right half of the image shows g1 and g2 combined using the `Show` command:

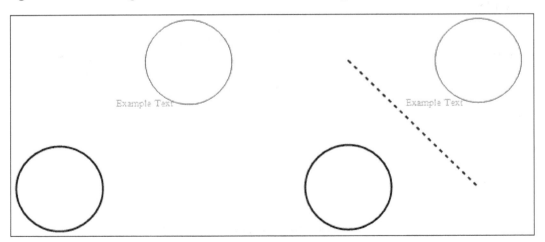

Figure 3.8 Basic primitives rendered using the Graphics function

The canvas adjusts its range to automatically include all the drawing elements, so we do not need to manually define the canvas area.

Adding interactivity – Dynamic and Refresh

As mentioned before, we will need to send the dynamically updating mouse coordinate positions to the mapCoordToInd function, and plot the zoom inset dynamically. In order to achieve this, we will write the rest of the code within a function called Dynamic. This is one possible way to achieve dynamic interactivity in Mathematica. The function updates the code or objects inside it dynamically, the refresh rate of which can be controlled using the Refresh function. Here is the rest of the code:

```
Dynamic[
  coords = MousePosition["GraphicsScaled"];
  coords2 = MousePosition["Graphics"];
  If[coords2 == None, coords2 = {0, 0}];
  Refresh[
    (* find date range *)
    inds = mapCoordToInd[ coords, Length[data] ];
    insetg = DateListPlot[ data[[ inds[[1]];;inds[[2]] ]],
AspectRatio->1/6, ImageSize->{500, 100} ];
    dlp = DateListPlot[ data, ImageSize->500, Filling->Bottom, Joined-
>True];

    Grid[{
      {insetg},
      {Show[ dlp,
Graphics[{Gray,Thick,Line[{{coords2[[1]],datamin},{coords2[[1]],datam
ax}}]} ]}
      ]} (* end of Show *)
    }], (* end of Grid *)
    UpdateInterval->1
  ] (* end of Refresh *)
] (* end of Dynamic *)
```

Inside the Dynamic function, we call the MousePosition function with two different arguments. The coords function stores the scaled value (between 0 and 1) of the mouse position in the graphics canvas, and coords2 store the unscaled mouse position. The coords2 function is validated with an If condition, in case the mouse pointer is not over the graphics canvas, and set to (0, 0). Next, we enter the Refresh function. The syntax for the Refresh function is Refresh[**expr, opt**], where expr is the expression that will be updated by the Dynamic function, and opt can be various options that set the nature of updating. In this case, we set opt to UpdateInterval -> 1, which updates expr every 1 second.

With the scaled mouse pointer coordinates in our hand, we use our `mapCoordToInd` function to obtain a range of indices for the zoom plot, and create and store the plot in the `insetg` variable. The `AspectRatio` is set to `1/6` so that the plot is somewhat flattened, and the plot size is set manually using the `ImageSize` option. Then, the main plot with the full range of data is created and stored in `dlp`.

Finally, we use the `Grid` function that takes in a 2D list to arrange our plots nicely. In the first row of the grid, we place `insetg`. In the second row, we use the `Show` function to combine the main plot, `dlp`, with the gray indicator line. The line object is rendered using the graphics package, it uses the plot boundaries we calculated initially, and the updating mouse coordinates to draw a vertical line on the main plot. As a result, the line moves with the mouse pointer. That's it!

Evaluate the cell containing this code and you will see the interactive tool in action. With this small tool, it is much easier to interactively zoom into different datasets. We can tweak the code to do the same thing with ListPlot and other similar plots. Just replace the `DateListPlot` command with a plot command of your choice, as long as the dataset is correctly formatted to comply with our `mapCoordToInd` function.

With very little code, we created our first interactive visualization tool. So far, we covered the basic essentials of time series visualization. It is time to look into other types of scientific datasets too. What comes naturally after time is space. The rest of the chapter will be devoted to the visualization of spatial scientific data.

Isocontour and molecular visualization

In *Chapter 1, Visualization as a Tool to Understand Data*, we introduced the concept of scalar field, which is just a mathematical term used to describe the position-based values of a scalar quantity. Let's recap the example given in *Chapter 1, Visualization as a Tool to Understand Data*. Pressure, temperature, potential, and other physical values are often associated with coordinates to quantify the spatial variation of the physical parameter. To measure the temperature of a big space, instead of taking a single reading at a certain position, it makes better sense to measure the temperature at different locations and present them in a sorted manner.

A discrete scalar field is a set of such coordinates — scalar tuples. In this section, we will demonstrate how to visualize contours from these datasets (and why they are useful). In an effort to maximize our exposure to scientific datasets, we will work with a protein molecule to build a molecular visualization tool — a prototype of professional tools that are used by scientists. The visualization will render the atoms present in the protein along with layers of electrostatic potential isocontours.

If you are not familiar with the physics of electrostatic fields, don't worry, as you really don't need to know. After all, our focus is to create isocontour visualization, not theoretical physics!

Introduction to isocontours

Let's start with a 2D scalar field for the sake of simplicity. We will create a mock scalar field in Mathematica, and visualize the isocontours with the field to understand what an isocontour really means. The code for the 2D scalar field is as follows:

```
(* 2d scalar field visualization *)
(* create a scalar field of the form {x, y, x^2+y^2}, the scalar value
at each coordinate is x^2+y^2. *)
sc2d = Flatten[ Table[{x, y, x^2+y^2}, {x,1,8},{y,1,5,0.5} ], 1 ];

(* divide by the maximum value of the scalar quantity to scale the
other scalar values to [0, 1] *)
sc2d[[ ;;, 3 ]] = sc2d[[ ;;, 3 ]] / Max[ sc2d[[ ;;, 3 ]] ];

(* visualize the scalar field, grayscale intensity of each point is
set according to the scalar value at that point *)
Scg = Graphics[ Table[{
GrayLevel[ sc2d[[i,3]] ], Disk[{sc2d[[i,1]], sc2d[[i,2]]}, 0.1]}, {i,
1, Length[sc2d] }] (* end of Table *)
] (* end of Graphics *)
```

Here, `sc2d` is a list that contains a 2D scalar field. Using the `Table` function, we created a list that has the form $\{\{ \{x_1, y_1, S_{11}\}, \{x_1, y_2, S_{12}\}, ...\}, \{ \{x_2, y_1, S_{21}\}, \{x_2, y_2, S_{22}\}, ...\}, ...\}$. Essentially, it is a 2D matrix of x and y values, with a scalar value S associated with each coordinate. Here, S is calculated using a simple formula, $S = x^2 + y^2$.

Next, we flatten the list to its first level, so we have a list that now looks like $\{ \{x_1, y_1, S_{11}\}, \{x_1, y_2, S_{12}\}, ..., \{x_2, y_1, S_{21}\}, \{x_2, y_2, S_{22}\}, ...\}$. Note that an extra level of curly brackets is now gone. This is done because the isocontour plot function requires the data in this format. The data here maintains a nice sequence in terms of x and y axes progression, but Mathematica's isocontour plot functions can also handle irregular point sets.

Then, we divide the scalar values by the maximum scalar value present in the data to scale all the values between 0 and 1. This is done to visualize the scalar value — we call the `Graphics` function to render a set of disks of radius 0.1, placed at the x and y positions mentioned in the scalar field, and set their color to a grayscale value (between 0 and 1). Once we have this graphic element stored in `scg`, we can plot the isocontours using the `ListContourPlot` function and show them together, as follows:

```
lcp = ListContourPlot[sc2d, AspectRatio->0.6, ColorFunction->
ColorData["Aquamarine"], Contours-> 4]
Show[lcp, scg]
```

The following screenshot shows what the outputs look like (left: `scg` and right: `lcp` and `scg` combined):

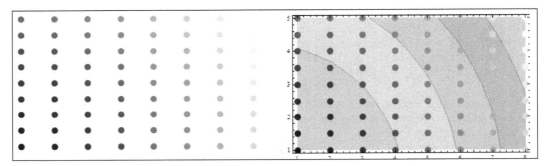

Figure 3.9 (left) Points are shaded according to their scalar values, and (right) contour plot and points are rendered together

The `ListContourPlot` function plots the isocontours of a scalar field. The syntax for this function is:

```
ListContourPlot[data, opts (Contours, …)],
```

Here, an essential option is `Contours`. It can be set either to the number of desired contours, or to specific contour values. Next, `scg` and `lcp` (the contour plot) are combined on the same plot using `Show`.

Let's take a moment to understand what is going on here. Our scalar field is represented visually in `scg`, where a higher grayscale value indicates a higher scalar value. Hence, we can infer from the figure that as we move from the lower left corner to the upper right corner, the scalar values associated with the points increase. The contour plot overlaid with `scg` shows the contours for this scalar field. Contours define the approximate areas where the scalar quantity remains the same. Notice the approximately similar grayscale values of any set of points that belong to the same shaded area.

Contours provide a quick way to figure out the spatial distribution of scalar values in a scalar field. Since they reveal groups of equal (iso) values, they are also called isocontours. It is harder to distinguish between values just by coloring the points according to the associated scalar value (as done in the case of scg). The isocontour plot shown in the preceding figure provides us a better way to judge the overall structure of the scalar field, without examining the points individually.

Example project – protein molecule visualization

Scientists who work in the fields of structural biology, drug design, or biophysics often use molecular dynamics simulations to understand the structure of proteins. In these simulations, an essential physical quantity of interest is the electrostatic potential field in and around the protein structure. This is essentially a scalar field, with electric potential values calculated at regularly spaced intervals within the volume, confined by the protein molecule.

In this project, we will pull together some of the concepts and functions discussed so far in this chapter, along with another new function, Manipulate, that replaces the Dynamic function to bring in a whole new level of interactivity. The scalar field data for the project is generated in the notebook ScalarFieldGeneration.nb.

The actual calculation of the field requires sophisticated mathematics, so the author, in an attempt to keep things simple, used a dummy mathematical model to generate the field. Interested readers are encouraged to read the code. It demonstrates the use of compiled functions and ParallelTable to speed up the calculations by several orders of magnitude. This is a good lesson for those who are also interested in big data and high performance computing with Mathematica.

For our project, we created three scalar field files using the code in ScalarFieldGeneration.nb, and saved them in the data folder of the Chapter3 code folder. Other than the scalar field data, we have a protein data file that is called 1CLL.pdb.

Our final prototype will look like the following screenshot:

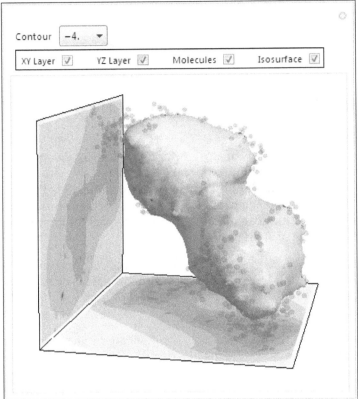

Figure 3.10 Protein molecule visualization tool

We will visualize the atoms present in the protein molecule as small transparent spheres. There will be two layers of 2D isocontours. These will show the overall structure of contours when the electrostatic potential field is projected on the x-y and y-z axes. Finally, we will render an isosurface, which is the three-dimensional version of isocontours. The surface will represent the points in 3D space that has the same potential, the potential value of interest being selectable from the drop-down menu named **Contour**. We will provide checkboxes to enable or disable rendering each of these elements in the visualization project.

Let's get started with the project.

Loading and visualizing the protein molecule

The protein structure we will investigate is called 1CLL in the protein database. A standard file format used in the scientific community to exchange protein information is .pdb. Mathematica provides native support to import this file format, so we will take advantage of this, instead of writing our own file format reader. As always, let's set our working directory first, using the following code:

```
SetDirectory[NotebookDirectory[]]
```

Next, we will import the pdb file using the following lines of code:

```
dat1 = Import["data/1CLL.pdb", "ResidueAtoms"];
dat2 = Import["data/1CLL.pdb", "ResidueCoordinates"];
```

This is a new form of Import, with an additional argument to define the fields we are interested in. If we write the following piece of code in a different cell, then Mathematica will list the table headers present in the data file:

```
Import[["data/1CLL.pdb", "Elements"];
```

We will see that the 1CLL.pdb file has several data header elements. Basically, these list the different tables of data that are integrated in the same file. As a second argument in the Import function, we can provide the name of the header to import the relevant table.

In this case, we will import the tables ResidueAtoms and ResidueCoordinates. These tables complement each other. ResidueAtoms has the list of atoms that make up the protein molecule, and for each row in this table, the corresponding row in ResidueCoordinates lists the $\{x, y, z\}$ position of the atom in the protein structure.

Let's also import the scalar field file at this point, using the following lines of code. One file is a 3D scalar field, which means that the ith row in the file has the format $\{x_i, y_i, z_i, E_i\}$, where E is the electrostatic potential value at the coordinate $\{x_i, y_i, z_i\}$. The other two files contain 2D scalar fields, similar to the structure we just dealt with for the 2D isocontour plot:

```
(* import the pre-calculated scalar field data *)
scfield = Import["data/sc3d_res100.csv"];
scxy = Import["data/scxy_res100.csv"];
scyz = Import["data/scyz_res100.csv"];
```

At this point, if we want to see the total number of atoms that we will be working with, we can do the following:

```
(* how many residue atoms in total? *)
Tally[ Flatten[dat1] ]
```

The output will be `{{N,182}, {C,694}, {O,247}, {S,9}, {Ca,4}, {H,1}}`. These are the counts for each type of residue atom that is present in the molecule. Next, using the following lines of code, let's clean up the dat1 and dat2 variables, getting rid of extra levels of brackets:

```
(* fldat2 will contain the 3D coordinates of each atom, fldat1 will
contain the element symbol of the corresponding atoms *)
fldat2 = Flatten[dat2, 2];
fldat1 = Flatten[dat1];
```

Now that we have the coordinates of each atom, and the atom names, let's visualize the position of these atoms using Graphics3D with the following code, which is just the 3D version of Graphics and is used for drawing 3D graphic primitives:

```
(* Create a table of graphics elements for all atoms *)
verttable = Table[
 { Opacity[0.2],
  Switch[ fldat1[[i]],
   "N", ColorData["Atoms"]["N"],
   "C", ColorData["Atoms"]["C"],
   "O", ColorData["Atoms"]["O"],
   "S", ColorData["Atoms"]["S"],
   "Ca", ColorData["Atoms"]["Ca"],
   "H", ColorData["Atoms"]["H"] ], (* end of Switch *)
  Sphere[ fldat2[[i]], 50 ] },
{i, 1, Length[fldat2]} ]; (* end of Table *)

(* visualize the atom positions *)
Graphics3D[verttable,Axes->True,AxesLabel->{X,Y,Z}]
```

Here, we create a list using the Table function, which will be passed on to Graphics3D, to draw spheres in the position of the atoms. Remember that Graphics or Graphics3D works using some primitive shape commands, but before placing the commands, we will need to define the style (color, size, and so on) for the graphic element.

In this case, a sample list will look like the parameter {Opacity[0.2], Red, Sphere[{x$_1$, y$_1$, z$_1$}, 50], Opacity[0.2], Blue, Sphere[{x$_2$, y$_2$, z$_2$}, 50]}. When this list is passed to Graphics3D, we will see two red and blue spheres of radius 50 units placed at {x_1, y_1, z_1} and {x_2, y_2, z_2}, almost transparent because of the stated opacity value. We want to do the same for all the atoms.

The functions fldat2 and fldat1 have the same number of members. So, we parse through both using the same Table function. The fldat1 function contains the name of the elements. For the *i*th element of this list, we use a Switch statement to determine the color of the graphic primitive, based on the name of the atom. The syntax Switch[**expr, form1, value1, form2, value2**, ...] takes in the test expression expr, and based on the possible values form$_i$ of this expression, evaluates and returns value$_i$. So, for each atom name, we return a particular color name. The color scheme presented here is based on Mathematica's own color scheme for atom names.

After we are done with the Switch statement, we include the sphere command and set the *i*th element of fldat2 as the sphere's coordinates. Thus, one element of the resulting list from this Table command will be {Opacity[0.2], (Color Name for Atom$_1$), Sphere[{x_1, y_1, z_1}, 50]}. This Table function will return a list containing similar sublists for each atom, which is then passed to the Graphics3D command. The following figure shows the output from the code:

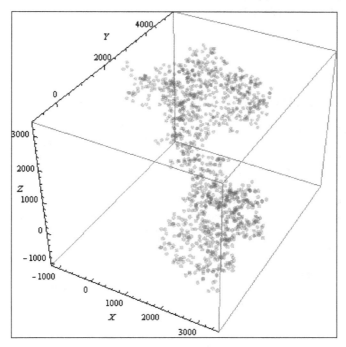

Figure 3.11 Rendering the protein molecule with semitransparent spheres

This is the physical structure of the residue atoms in the protein 1CLL. For later visualization purposes, let's store this graphic element in a variable in the following code, without the box and axes:

```
coordvis = Graphics3D[verttable, Axes-> False, Boxed-> False];
```

Here is what we will do next. At regular-spaced intervals inside the preceding bounding box, we already calculated the combined potential due to the whole group of atoms. This is saved in the 3D scalar field, `scfield`. The other two scalar fields, `scxy` and `scyz`, contain the 2D scalar fields that are the potential fields for the *x-y* and *y-z* planes (refer to the screenshot of the visualization, figure 3.10, for details). We will generate the contour plots (both 3D and 2D), and combine them using the `Show` command. To combine the 2D plots in a 3D space, we need to embed them as textures in polygons.

Preparing the isocontour plots

We need to know the bounding box of the atoms that we visualized previously. This is done by parsing through `fldat2` for each axis and finding the minimum and maximum values, as done in the following lines of code:

```
minx = Min[fldat2[[;;,1]]]
miny = Min[fldat2[[;;,2]]]
minz = Min[fldat2[[;;,3]]]
maxx = Max[fldat2[[;;,1]]]
maxy = Max[fldat2[[;;,2]]]
maxz = Max[fldat2[[;;,3]]]
```

Next, we will plot the 2D isocontours and store them as graphics:

```
lpxy = ListContourPlot[scxy, ContourShading->Automatic, ColorFunction-
>ColorData["CoffeeTones"], ContourStyle->None, Frame->False]
lpyz = ListContourPlot[scyz, ContourShading->Automatic, ColorFunction-
>"BlueGreenYellow", ContourStyle->None, Frame->False]
```

In order to embed these plots as textures in a polygon, we create a polygon with four points in the 3D space, using the appropriate minimum and maximum bounds as the coordinates of the polygons to ensure that they are big enough in the final visualization:

```
glpxy = Graphics3D[ {White, Texture[lpxy], Polygon[{{minx,miny,minz},
{maxx,miny,minz}, {maxx,maxy,minz}, {minx,maxy,minz}},
VertexTextureCoordinates-> {{0,0,0},{1,0,0},{1,1,0},{0,1,0}}]}, Boxed-
>False, Lighting->"Neutral"]
```

We set the `Texture` property of the `Polygon` shape (defined within `Graphics3D`) to the plot image we just created, which is `lpxy`. Then, for the *x-y* plane, the appropriate axes bounds are chosen as the polygon coordinates. The `VertexTextureCoordinates` function ensures that we map the corners of the image to the correct corners of the polygon. The 3D lighting property of `Graphics3D` is set to neutral so that no shadows are created. The same code is written for the *y-z* axes isocontour visualization, except with different bounds, shown as follows:

```
glpyz = Graphics3D[ {Texture[lpyz], Polygon[{{minx,miny,m
inz},{minx,maxy,minz},{minx,maxy,maxz},{minx,miny,maxz}},
VertexTextureCoordinates->{{0,0,0},{1,0,0},{1,1,0},{0,1,0}}]},
Boxed->False, Lighting->"Neutral"]
```

The following figure shows the polygons generated using the preceding code:

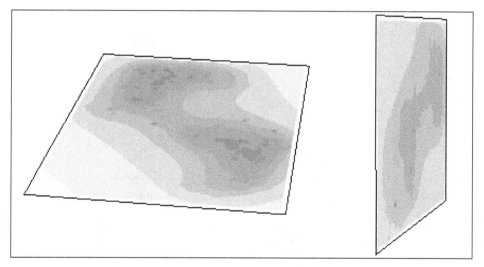

Figure 3.12 2D isocontour plots of the potential field

Adding interactivity – manipulate

In the rest of the code, we will gather all of the above graphic variables under one construct using `Show`. However, instead of `Dynamic`, we will use `Manipulate`.

The `Manipulate` function is a wonderful Mathematica function to integrate interactivity with our visualizations. The basic syntax is:

```
Manipulate[ expr,{u, umin, umax }]
```

Here, u is a variable that can be used inside expr. Based on the minimum and maximum values of u, Mathematica will present us with an interactive panel to interact with whatever expression we put as expr. For example, take the following code snippet:

```
Manipulate[x,{x,1,10}]
Manipulate[ Graphics[{GrayLevel[x],Disk[]}], {{x,0.1,"Grayscale"},
{0.1,0.5,0.7}} ]
```

This code will produce interactive panels as shown in the following screenshot:

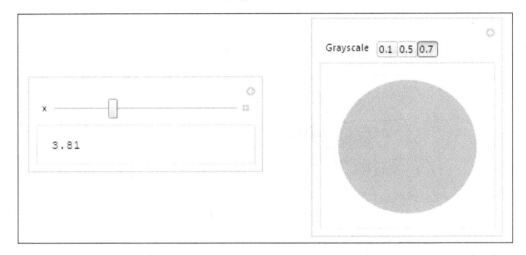

Figure 3.13 (left) simple Manipulate example, and (right) controlling the fill of a circle in Manipulate

For the first panel (left), we only defined the minimum and maximum values of x. After evaluation, Manipulate provided us with a drag panel to change the value of x. Instead of defining a range, if we define a set of values (along with an initial value and label for the variable, for example, {x, 0.1, "Grayscale"}, it sets the x value to 0.1 initially, and labels the variable with the string "Grayscale"), then Manipulate will provide us with list of values to choose from (right).

We will use Manipulate in a similar way to create the final visualization.

Isosurface and styling

The rest of the code using Manipulate is as follows:

```
Manipulate[
 Show[
  If[layer1,glpxy,{}],
```

```
    If[layer2,glpyz,{}],
    If[isosurface, ListContourPlot3D[scfield, Contours->{conts}, Mesh-
>None, ContourStyle->{Opacity[0.8]}, PlotRange->All, ColorFunction-
>"Aquamarine", Boxed->False, MaxPlotPoints->40], {}],
    If[molecules,coordvis,{}],
    Lighting->"Neutral",
    Boxed->False,
    Axes->False
  ], (* end of Show function *)
  {{conts,-4.2,"Contour"},Table[i,{i,-4.6,-3,0.2}]},
  Row[{Control[{{layer1,True,"XY Layer"},{True,False}}],
  Control[{{layer2,True,"YZ Layer"},{True,False}}],
  Control[{{molecules,True,"Molecules"},{True,False}}],
  Control[{{isosurface,True,"Isosurface"},{True,False}}] },
  Spacer[20], Frame->True] (* end of Row *)
] (* end of Manipulate *)
```

The brackets can be a little difficult to trace, so I recommend taking a look at the code inside Mathematica, since it offers bracket highlighting. There can be multiple panel variables in Manipulate (unlike a single variable x, such as the basic examples given in the previous code). In our case, we only need checkboxes for four Boolean variables and a combo box to select the desired isovalue for the isosurface. If the Boolean value for the checkbox variable is True, then we decide to show the respective graphic element. This is done within the Show with If conditionals. The four Booleans are isosurface, layer1, layer2, and molecules. Inside Show, we check each of them in turn, and return the previously calculated graphic elements if they are checked.

The isosurface plot is created on the go using the ListContourPlot3D function. It has the same syntax as ListContourPlot, except that it has $\{x, y, z, E\}$ as the input list format, instead of $\{x, y, E\}$. The contour to render is selected from the variable conts (Contours -> {conts}), which is just another control/panel variable under Manipulate. We defined the values explicitly for this variable (using a list of values generated using Table), so Manipulate will create a combobox for this variable. The other option worth mentioning is MaxPlotPoints. Setting MaxPlotPoints to a finite number (lower than the total number of points in the calculated isosurface mesh) will increase the speed of rendering the scene. However, the shape of the isosurface will not be very accurate if a very low number is chosen.

The checkboxes governing the Boolean values are declared using the Control function. The syntax is Control[u, dom], where dom is the domain for the control. In this case, our domain is only True and False, which helps Mathematica understand that these are checkboxes. They are organized inside a function named Row, which keeps them separated. The separation value is set using the Spacer option.

Evaluate the cell to see the visualization in action (the figure shown at the beginning of the project). The 3D scene can be rotated to view from different angles.

Thinking like a visualization scientist – isovalue analysis

Using this tool, we can view different isosurfaces for different isovalues. Usually, it is not obvious what isovalues we should choose to see the different properties of scalar fields. In such cases, the histogram of all possible isovalues present in the scalar fields can be used as a guide, as shown in the following screenshot:

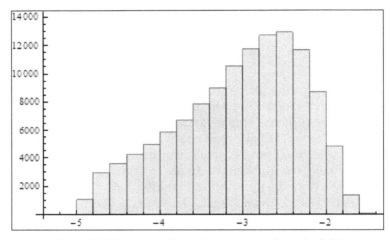

Figure 3.14 Histogram of isovalues present in the scalar field

In the histogram in figure 3.14 (generated using the `Histogram[]` function, to be introduced in the next chapter), there is a peak at around -2.5. This means that a lot of points in the scalar field volume have an isovalue of -2.5. Scientists are mostly interested to see the isosurface shape within and near the molecule. An isovalue closer to the peak will only yield the isosurfaces that occupy a larger area in the bounding box; for an electrostatic potential field, it is likely that such isosurfaces will enclose unnecessarily bigger volumes around the protein.

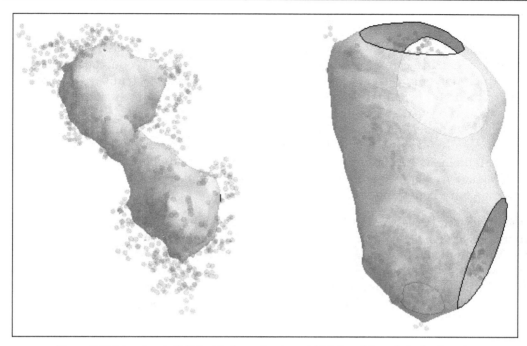

Figure 3.15 Isosurface is (left) inside the molecule and (right) too big to fit in the domain

The isovalue -4.2 yields an isosurface that occupies less volume and is within the protein molecule region (left). However, an isovalue of -3.2 (closer to the peak) encloses a bigger volume and is not very interesting. The holes are created because the scalar field was not calculated beyond the bounding box of the molecule.

This example demonstrates that along with the visualization tool we create, some data hacking and trial-and-error is required to turn our tool into an effective visualization tool.

Further reading

The research literature in time series visualization and scientific visualization is vast. We only learned about the main techniques that Mathematica offers to visualize our data, but the design and aesthetics issues are equally (or more) important. *The Visualization Handbook, Charles D. Hansen* and *Chris R. Johnson, Academic Press,* lists detailed methods of isosurface and other scientific visualization algorithms. Time series visualization designs are discussed in many books. A survey of different designs can be found at the link http://survey.timeviz.net/.

Summary

In this chapter, we actually covered a lot of ground to create interactive visualizations. Starting with periodic time series visualization, we built a small zoom tool to aid the exploration of time series. In the process, we made ourselves familiar with the `Dynamic` and `Refresh` functions—our first step in Mathematica interactivity. We then concentrated on spatial data visualization, specifically isocontours in 2D and 3D. The molecular visualization tool demonstrates the practical use of isocontours in the real world. We also introduced ourselves to `Manipulate`, the widely used function that helps Mathematica programmers create interactive applications. Our encounter with `Manipulate` was brief, but we will cover it in more detail in the next chapter so that you can gain a better understanding of this package.

It is important to realize that Mathematica provides the necessary plotting tools and functions to visualize our data, but instead of sticking to traditional plots and charts, we can do much more using this powerful language if we are willing to employ custom designs in our visualizations. The goal of the book is to teach you to do this. Hence, in the next chapter, we will focus on a few mini projects that deal with some other kinds of information. Through the development of these projects, we will learn more advanced techniques to create custom and interactive tools.

4
Statistical and Information Visualization

The word *information* can be used to define a broad range of knowledge and knowledge-based inference. In the context of our book, information visualization refers to the techniques of visualizing different kinds of dataset that we have introduced in *Chapter 1, Visualization as a Tool to Understand Data*. Even though time series and scientific data are also information, we have separated the previous chapter from the current one in order to respect the current categorization of research in the visualization community. Scientific visualization practitioners tend to deal with datasets that arise specifically in the context of scientific experiments or simulations, whereas information visualization practitioners have traditionally focused their research on other kinds of widely used data, such as text, graph networks, statistical plots, maps, and so on.

In this chapter, we will play with the capabilities of Mathematica to visualize statistical, text, and graph networks data. We will learn about some of the basic and essential statistical plot functions. As an example project, we will write some code to demonstrate some computational statistics concepts and the corresponding visualization in Mathematica. Also, by the end of this chapter, we should be confident and comfortable in handling both text and graph networks data, each section leading to its own mini project. Through the projects in the chapter, we will touch on some essential concepts of visualization theory.

Statistical visualization

Mathematica provides us with a wide variety of statistical plotting functions. Let's take a look at a few of them:

- Distribution shapes
  - Histogram
  - SmoothHistogram
  - Histogram3D
  - PairedHistogram
  - DensityHistogram and so on
- Charting
  - PieChart
  - BubbleChart
  - BarChart
  - SectorChart
  - PairedBarChart
  - 3D versions of some of these charts
- Miscellaneous
  - Gauges, such as AngularGauge, HorizontalGauge, VerticalGauge, BulletGauge, ClockGauge, and so on
  - Financial charts, such as CandlestickChart, TradingChart, FinancialIndicator, KagiChart, RenkoChart, and so on

To visualize the distribution shapes of empirical data, Mathematica provides different kinds of histogram-plotting functions. SmoothHistogram provides a smooth estimation of the shape, whereas Histogram, Histogram3D, and PairedHistogram give a discrete shape (which is often better to understand empirical data). DensityHistogram is a plot for visualizing spatial data density.

The most common charting functions are listed next. We have already used SectorChart to visualize periodic time series data. PairedBarChart is used to display two sets of bar charts together for a side-by-side comparison, much like the PairedHistogram.

Other than the standard plotting and charting, Mathematica has some miscellaneous visualization functions. Gauges and meters are useful for creating progress bars and similar range-specific information. Coupled with `Dynamic` or `Manipulate`, we can create various interactive visualizations. Financial charts provide some charting functions that are useful for finance analysts and quantitative researchers.

The miscellaneous functions are used less often. So, we will demonstrate some more common plotting functions in this section. The readers who are interested in learning more about other functions can look up the Mathematica documentation.

The swiss bank notes dataset

For some of the examples in this chapter, we will use the swiss bank notes dataset available in the example data repository of Mathematica. This dataset contains the margin and diagonal measurements of 200 swiss bank notes, of which 100 are genuine, and the other 100 are counterfeit. In the following code, the function `ExampleData` is used to load this dataset:

```
ExampleData[{"Statistics","SwissBankNotes"},"LongDescription"]
ExampleData[{"Statistics","SwissBankNotes"},"ColumnDescriptions"]
data = ExampleData[{"Statistics","SwissBankNotes"}];
```

The first line of code specifies the dataset we want to load, and pulls out the description given for the dataset. The `ExampleData` function's first argument specifies the dataset, and the second (optional) argument defines any information attributable to the dataset. In the third line, we actually load the dataset into the list `data`.

The output from the first two lines of the code is as follows:

```
Six measurements made on 100 genuine Swiss bank notes and 100
counterfeit ones.
{Length of bill in mm, Width of left edge in mm, Width of right edge
in mm, Bottom margin width in mm, Top margin width in mm, Length of
image diagonal in mm, Genuine 0 or counterfeit 1}
```

The column descriptions are self-explanatory. An example entry of the dataset is shown in the following code:

```
{214.8, 131, 131.1, 9, 9.7, 141, 0}
```

This particular dataset provides a chance to demonstrate the power of data visualization applied to a real-world problem—which is to distinguish the cluster of genuine notes from the counterfeit cluster, relying entirely on the margin measurements without the 0-1 labeling. This will be covered in the section on similarity mapping. For now, let's get back to statistical plots.

Histograms and charts

One of the attractive features of Mathematica is its integrity and ease of syntax. Most of the plotting functions do not really require any tutorial once the user figures out the input data format that the plotting function requires. This is just an *F1* key-press away, as the comprehensive Mathematica documentation lists all the possible syntax and options of the function right away. The rest of the styling and beautification are done by defining some of the properties of the plots and charts, most of which are commonly shared between the different plot functions. Hence, instead of listing an example for each of the previous plots, we are going to pick a few examples to give us a feeling of the possible usage scenarios of these plots. The saved page space will be devoted to more exciting visualization adventures with interesting datasets!

Histogram

The Histogram function draws a histogram, which is the most used plot in statistics, from a list of data (or several lists of data, overlaying the different histograms on the same plot). The basic syntax is simple, and is as follows:

```
Histogram[data, bspec, options…]
```

Here, data is a list of numbers, bspec is the number of bins, and options are the styling properties for the histogram. Other than data, the rest of the arguments are optional. For plotting multiple datasets, we will use the following syntax:

```
Histogram[{data₁, data₂…}, bspec, options…]
```

Let's use the bank notes dataset to demonstrate some histograms:

```
(* histogram of bottom margin widths *)
Histogram[ data[[;;,4]], 20]
```

This will result in the following figure:

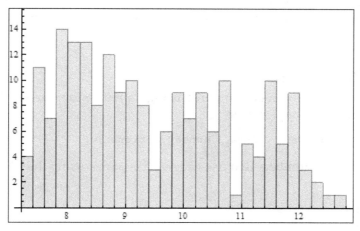

Figure 4.1 A histogram of bottom margin widths

We have selected all rows that contain the fourth column, which will give us a list of numbers that contain the bottom margin widths. We have also specified the number of bins as 20. As shown in figure 4.1, the bank notes have a good variety of bottom margin widths. Let's compare the bottom margins with the top margins by plotting multiple histograms on the same plot using the following lines of code:

```
(* multiple plots and styling *)
Histogram[{ data[[;;,4]], data[[;;,5]] }, 20, Frame->True, FrameLabel-
>{"Bottom/Top Margin Width (mm)","Frequency"}]
```

The output of this code is shown in the following screenshot:

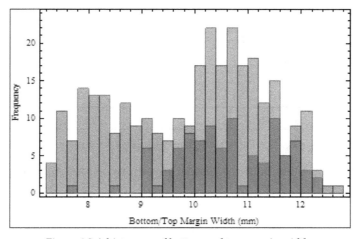

Figure 4.2 A histogram of bottom and top margin widths

Mathematica chooses different colors to distinguish between the histograms automatically, unless we define our own colors. In the preceding figure, we have included a frame and set the frame labels for the horizontal and vertical axes using the `FrameLabel` option.

PairedHistogram

The two sets of numbers can be compared using PairedHistogram too. The syntax for `PairedHistogram` is as follows:

```
PairedHistogram[data₁, data₂, bspec, options…]
```

Let's compare sets of numbers that use `PairedHistogram` using the following code snippet:

```
(* paired histograms *)
PairedHistogram[ data[[;;,4]], data[[;;,5]], 20 ]
```

The number of bins is set to 20 again. This output can be seen in the following screenshot:

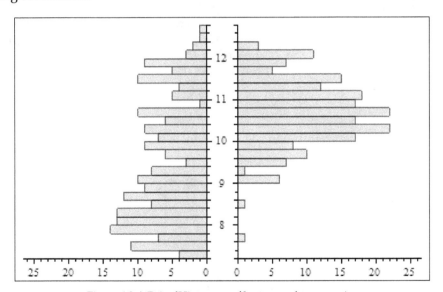

Figure 4.3 A PairedHistogram of bottom and top margins

The paired histogram plots both the histograms on two sides for bin-specific comparison.

Histogram3D

This function can be used to visualize the distribution of random variables that have two dimensions. The syntax for this function is as follows:

```
Histogram3D[{ {x₁,y₁}, {x₂,y₂}, ... }, bspec, options...]
```

Here, each element of the list is now a list of two numbers. Let's demonstrate the function using some randomly generated data using the following code:

```
(* 3d histogram example *)
data1 = RandomVariate[ NormalDistribution[0,1], {1000,2}];
data2 = RandomVariate[ NormalDistribution[3,0.7], {1000,2}];
Histogram3D[{data1,data2}]
```

Here, RandomVariate is a function that creates a set of random numbers based on the distribution entered in its first argument. The second argument seeks the dimension of the randomly generated list. For both the data series, we have chosen the normal distribution, one with a mean of 0 and standard deviation of 1, the other with a mean of 3 and standard deviation of 0.7 (thus, narrower and taller). Both datasets are of dimension 1,000 by 2, which means there are 1,000 rows, each containing 2 random numbers. Next, we pass both the datasets to Histogram3D. Figure 4.4 shows the result as follows:

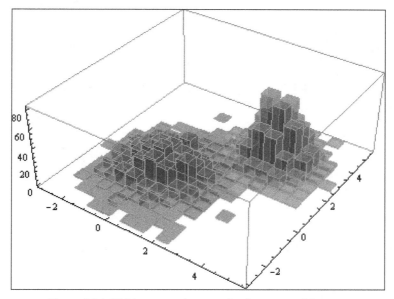

Figure 4.4 A 3D histogram of two randomly generated datasets

The resulting figure can be tilted and rotated in Mathematica to explore the shape of the distributions.

PieChart

The pie chart is a way to show the percentage occupation of different variables in the same space according to their magnitudes. The advantage of plotting a pie chart in Mathematica is the interactivity and labeling capabilities this function provides. Each slice in the pie chart can be clicked to distinguish it from the rest of the slices. The `LabelingFunction` property also provides several options to manage the slice labels, as shown in the following code snippet:

```
(* pie chart *)
data3 = RandomVariate[ NormalDistribution[1,0.5], 30];
PieChart[ data3, ChartStyle->"CoffeeTones", ChartLabels->Table[i,
{i,30}], LabelingFunction->"RadialCallout"]
```

In this case, we have generated a random list that contains 30 numbers. The `PieChart` function is called with several other styling options. The `ChartStyle` option sets a different color map. The `ChartLabels` option takes in a list of labels to label each slice. In this case, we have only provided a list of numbers going from 1 to 30, labeling each number in the random list with their respective sequence. The `LabelingFunction` option is set to the value `"RadialCallout"` to show an extra layer of labels that state the actual values at the periphery of the chart, as shown in the following screenshot:

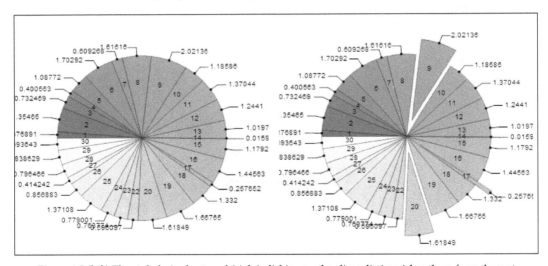

Figure 4.5 (left) The styled pie chart, and (right) clicking on the slices distinguishes them from the rest

BubbleChart

The bubble chart is a nice way to visualize numerical datasets that have three dimensions. We can think of it as an extended version of ListPlot, where we plot points at (x, y) coordinates, but instead of drawing equally sized points, we draw filled circles, the radii of which represent magnitude values. This is perfect for visualizing data that have a magnitude component associated with the (x, y) coordinates. Let's look at the syntax and an example:

```
BubbleChart[{{x₁,y₁,z₁}, {x₂,y₂,z₂}, …}, options…]
```

The function takes in a dataset whose elements are each a tuple of three numbers. The first two numbers define the x and y coordinates of the point in the plotting space, and the third number defines a magnitude, and dictates the radius of the filled circle at that point:

```
(* bubble chart *)
data4 = RandomVariate[ NormalDistribution[1,0.5], {30,3}];
BubbleChart[ data4, ChartStyle->"GrayTones"]
```

We create a randomly generated list of 50 tuples that have three numbers. The BubbleChart function simply takes the data and plots them with the ChartStyle option set to the GrayTones color map. The following figure 4.6 shows the result:

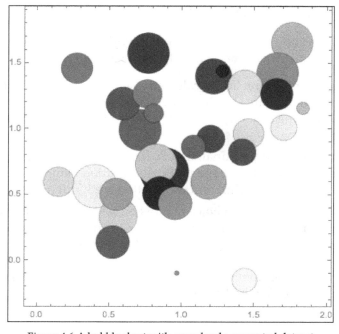

Figure 4.6 A bubble chart with a randomly generated dataset

If you have dabbled around the world of visualization for a while, then you must have heard of Hans Rosling, and watched his famous lecture on the evolution of poverty. In his lectures, he uses an interactive bubble chart to demonstrate how life expectancy and income vary for different countries as their population changes. This is nothing but a series of bubble charts with life expectancy in the vertical axis, GDP/capita in the horizontal axis, and population size of countries (points in the graph) acting as the magnitude associated with the 2D coordinates.

 As an exercise, you can visit the Gapminder software website at `http://www.gapminder.org/downloads/` to download the data from Hans Rosling's talks, and replicate the same interactive animation using `BubbleChart` and `Manipulate` in Mathematica.

Choosing appropriate plots

We have demonstrated a few statistical plotting capabilities of Mathematica. In the previous chapters, we also saw some other plotting packages in action. By now, we should have a better intuition on the types of plots, the input data formats, and the styling options that are available to us. At this point, a natural and very important question that we should be asking ourselves is the following: given a numeric dataset and a computer installed with Mathematica, what plots should we be using to investigate and dissect the dataset?

This is a difficult question and the answer varies widely based on the type of data. However, here are some tricks that will help us decide our plots:

- It is always a good practice to calculate the standard statistical quantities such as mean, median, standard deviation, minimum and maximum range, and so on, among other things; this helps us decide between normal and log-scale plotting.

- If the data is low-dimensional, that is, it is limited to two or three columns, then taking a look at the shape of the distribution using a histogram (or 3D histogram) may reveal different modes that are hidden in the data.

- We can narrow down our choice of plots by asking which dimensions (columns) of the data are of more importance. In some cases, we can find this by calculating correlations between different columns of the data. Then, depending on the nature of the data (spatial and time series) and the number of important dimensions, we can map each of those dimensions to an attribute of a plot, and decide whether the plot will be suitable.

- For communicating inferences to people from all backgrounds, it is better not to use fancy and complicated plots. Pie charts, line graphs, bubble charts, stacked charts, and others are good enough in many cases. Fancy plots are useful for technical people who are actually investigating and playing around with the data.

- Color maps are very important in any plot. We will talk a little bit on how to choose a better color map in *Chapter 5, Maps and Aesthetics*.

A glimpse of high-dimensional data

The traditional statistical plots yield a lot of useful information in general. However, as we have seen before, depending on the nature of the investigation, we may want to employ custom visualization techniques. Also, other than traditional statistics, we might as well touch upon computational statistics and the visualization tools that are useful in machine learning and high-dimensional data analysis.

Often, datasets have more than three or four columns, and we don't have the spatial or cognitive ability to visualize more dimensions. In these cases, we usually project the higher-dimensional data to some lower-dimensional space to compare and visualize them. One such visualization is known as similarity mapping. In this section, we will discuss the basic concepts of similarity mapping, and demonstrate how it can be used to visualize the clusters of counterfeit and genuine notes in the swiss bank notes dataset.

Similarity maps

For this exercise, we do not need to have any previous knowledge of complicated mathematics or computational statistics techniques. The idea is simple — we want to visualize the comparison of high-dimensional vectors. Assume we are given a numeric dataset with n columns and m rows. This means that we have n dimensions, or n features, and we have m observations that have these features. Each row (an observation) can be treated as a vector, where the number of elements in each vector is n.

We cannot possibly visualize these vectors. Instead, we can compare them with each other, and see how they differ on a global scale. A similarity map represents a matrix of size m by m (m rows and m columns), and each (i, j) entry in the matrix contains a number that defines a distance between the ith and jth indexed vectors in the dataset. The similarity maps are usually symmetric, since we use a distance measure that gives the same distance between ith and jth vectors, and jth and ith vectors.

The swiss bank notes dataset has six features (excluding the genuine/counterfeit labels) in six columns. Each row represents the measurements of an individual note. We would like to compare these properties of the bank notes, and plot the similarity map of these notes in order to check whether the genuine notes can be distinguished from the counterfeit ones.

Projecting information to low dimensions

Our goal is to calculate the distance between each pair of vectors in the dataset. There are many distance metrics available to calculate the distance between vectors, for example Euclidean, Squared Euclidean, Manhattan, Mahalanobis, Minkowski (which is really a generalization of Euclidean and Manhattan distance), and others. For our purpose, we will use the good old Euclidean metric to calculate the distance between each pair of vectors. In case of n features, the Euclidean distance formula for two vectors a and b is as follows:

```
Sqrt[(a_1 - b_1)^2 + (a_2 - b_2)^2 + (a_3 - b_3)^2 + ... + (a_n - b_n)^2]
```

Here, a_1, ..., an and b_1, ..., b_n represent the individual features of the vectors.

Note that by calculating the distance (a single number) between two high-dimensional vectors, we essentially reduce the amount of information. Now, we have a better control on the dimensionality. A set of numbers that represents the scalar distances between a set of vectors is easier to handle from a visualization perspective.

Visualizing genuine and counterfeit clusters

We will use the function `MatrixPlot` to visualize the actual similarity matrix. By virtue of Mathematica, the code is really short and simple. Let's get started with the following code:

```
ex = ExampleData[{"Statistics","SwissBankNotes"}];
ex = ex[[ Ordering[ ex[[;;,7]] ] ]] [[;;,1;;6]];
tb = Table[ EuclideanDistance[ ex[[i]], ex[[j]] ], {i,1,Length[ex]},
{j,1,Length[ex]} ];
```

The first line loads the dataset into the list `ex`. Next, we order the list according to the genuine (0) and counterfeit (1) labels. After ordering, we extract all rows, but take the first to sixth columns, leaving out the seventh column (genuine or counterfeit labels) so that they do not affect the distance between the feature vectors. Next, we simply calculate the Euclidean distance (using Mathematica's own function) between every possible pair of vectors and store the result in `tb`. The nested loops in the table run from 1 to the length of `ex`.

Next, all we need to do is visualize the similarity matrix `tb` using `MatrixPlot`, as shown in the following code:

```
MatrixPlot[ tb, ColorFunction->ColorData["GrayTones"]]
```

The output of this code snippet is shown in the following screenshot:

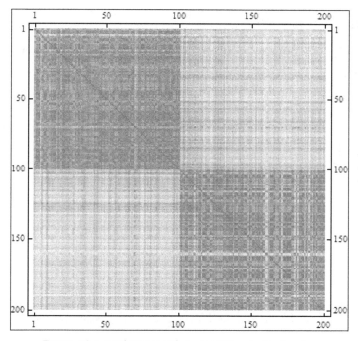

Figure 4.7 A similarity map between 200 swiss bank notes

The similarity map is a 200 by 200 matrix, where each entry (a pixel in the map) represents a distance value (color coded) between the respective ith and jth index. Notice the symmetric pattern across the diagonal. The color map `GrayTones` is a grayscale gradient color palette that indicates dark for low numbers and lighter for higher numbers. In the preceding map, the diagonal has the darkest color. It is because along the diagonal, each feature vector was compared to itself, so the distance between the two feature vectors was 0.

Also note the distinct clusters that formed between two different distance groups. The first 100 bank notes are genuine, and the Euclidean distances between their feature vectors are close to 0 (the dark square at the top left quadrant). This means they have similar features. Similarly, the notes between 100 and 200 have similar features too (dark square at the bottom right quadrant). However, there is a noticeable dissimilarity (bigger distance between feature vectors, hence lighter gray) between the two clusters of genuine and counterfeit notes.

As data visualization detectives, we should certainly dig a little deeper. A histogram of all distance values reveals that there is indeed a bimodal-shaped distribution. One mode is due to the smaller distances (both genuine and counterfeit notes that are similar within their own group), and the other mode is due to longer distances (when genuine was compared to counterfeit, or vice versa):

```
Histogram[ Flatten[tb], 20, FrameLabel->{"Euclidean Distance",
"Frequency"}, Frame->True]
```

The output of this code snippet is shown in the following screenshot:

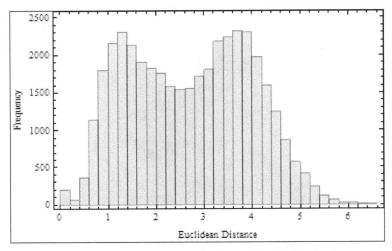

Figure 4.8 The list of distance values has a bimodal distribution

Similarity map for smaller datasets

Often, similarity maps are used to express similarity (or dissimilarity) in a smaller group of objects. In the previous example, we used the similarity map to look at the macro-level similarity behavior of the bank notes. The same concept can be polished to compare a handful of observations concisely. Imagine visualizing the similarity between a few countries' GDP, or comparing the yearly expenditure of 10 states. A nice way to capture all possible comparisons is to use similarity maps.

Let's write a bit more code to create one such visualization. Assume that we are only given 10 different bank notes' measurements, and we would like to compare the notes with each other. We are going to build the following visualization:

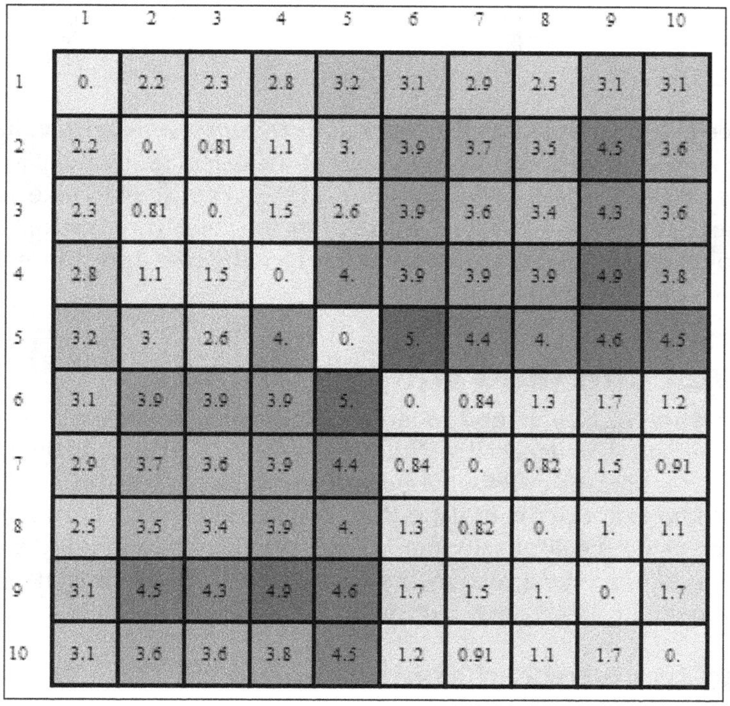

	1	2	3	4	5	6	7	8	9	10
1	0.	2.2	2.3	2.8	3.2	3.1	2.9	2.5	3.1	3.1
2	2.2	0.	0.81	1.1	3.	3.9	3.7	3.5	4.5	3.6
3	2.3	0.81	0.	1.5	2.6	3.9	3.6	3.4	4.3	3.6
4	2.8	1.1	1.5	0.	4.	3.9	3.9	3.9	4.9	3.8
5	3.2	3.	2.6	4.	0.	5.	4.4	4.	4.6	4.5
6	3.1	3.9	3.9	3.9	5.	0.	0.84	1.3	1.7	1.2
7	2.9	3.7	3.6	3.9	4.4	0.84	0.	0.82	1.5	0.91
8	2.5	3.5	3.4	3.9	4.	1.3	0.82	0.	1.	1.1
9	3.1	4.5	4.3	4.9	4.6	1.7	1.5	1.	0.	1.7
10	3.1	3.6	3.6	3.8	4.5	1.2	0.91	1.1	1.7	0.

Figure 4.9 A similarity map between 10 different bank notes

With a different color map, the table looks more appealing and presentable. In the case of this color map, darker blue means a bigger value. The text overlays and the row and column headers are added using the Graphics package. Let's start by choosing a smaller set of data from the original 200 rows in the following code:

```
ex2 = Join[ ex[[1;;5]], ex[[-5;;Length[ex]]], 1];
tb2 = Table[ EuclideanDistance[ ex2[[i]], ex2[[j]] ],
{i,1,Length[ex2]}, {j,1,Length[ex2]}];
```

Here, we have created a second set of data, joining the first five and the last five entries from ex (hence, five genuine and five counterfeit notes). Then, we create the similarity/distance matrix just like before and store it in tb2. Next, we combine the MatrixPlot with a nice color map and text overlays using the following lines of code:

```
Show[
MatrixPlot[ tb2, ColorFunction->ColorData["RedBlueTones"], Frame-
>False, Mesh->All, MeshStyle->Thick],
Graphics[ Table[ Text[ NumberForm[tb2[[i,j]], 2], {j-0.5, 10.5-i}],
{i,1,Length[ex2]}, {j,1,Length[ex2]}] ],
```

```
Graphics[ Table[ Text[11-i, {-0.5, i-0.5}], {i,1,10} ] ] ,
Graphics[ Table[ Text[i, {i-0.5, 10.5}], {i,1,10}] ]
]
```

There are three text overlays. The first overlay is the actual distance values on each cell. The `NumberForm` function is used to restrict the calculated values to two digits, and the text is placed at the coordinates ($j - 0.5$, $10.5 - i$) to take account of the origin that starts at (0, 0), since `MatrixPlot` plots the cells from the top-left corner. The other two `Graphics` elements are used to place the row and column headers in a similar fashion.

Things that can (and will) go wrong

A data visualization ninja is bound to face challenges when investigating a large dataset. This is inevitable, especially if they are working with it for the first time. There are pitfalls and traps everywhere due to the way we use our available tools. The problem is not in the tools; rather, it is in their usage. Let's look at two demonstrations using the similarity maps we just built. Keep in mind that these problems are not specific to similarity mapping only; these are mistakes that we unknowingly make unless we are cautious.

Employing the wrong distance metric

As mentioned before, there are a lot of different distance metrics available to compare numeric data in low and high dimensions. Before we pick one, we should experiment enough, at least on smaller datasets, to find out whether it meets our needs.

For example, a metric to compare high-dimensional vectors is to find the cosine of the angle between the vectors. This can be calculated by taking the dot product of the two vectors and dividing it by the product of their magnitudes. Figure 4.10 shows the resulting similarity map and the distribution of the cosine values:

```
tb = Table[ Dot[ ex[[i]], ex[[j]] ] / ( Norm[ ex[[i]] ] * Norm[
ex[[j]] ] ), {i,1,Length[ex]}, {j,1,Length[ex]}]
```

The output of this code is shown in the following screenshot:

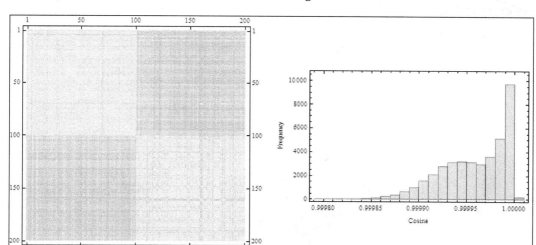

Figure 4.10 (left) A similarity map using the cosine metric, (right) and the distribution of cosine values

Notice that the clusters are not as distinct as the previous map; the darker values are less pronounced. This is mostly because the similarity values are now jammed close to 1, so the GrayTones color map puts most of the values on the lighter side of the scale. Looking at the distribution, we realize that it is not quite bimodal, which defeats the purpose of clustering the two different labels.

Choosing a misleading color map

A widely used color map, since the early days of visualization, is the rainbow color map. It is present in Mathematica as one of the gradient color palettes. The problem of choosing such a widely varying color map will be discussed in *Chapter 5, Maps and Aesthetics*. Just to provide some context here, let's examine figure 4.11 that shows our original similarity map rendered with a rainbow color map. There are three distinct colors that one can notice here—shades of green, yellow, and red. Without a specific guideline for color variation, it is hard to compare the nature of intermediate distance values.

A grayscale color map has a uniform evolution from darker to lighter shades, so it is easier to understand the transitions.

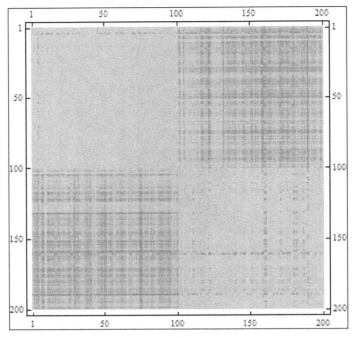

Figure 4.11 A rainbow color map can be misleading due to multiple colors used to represent a single dimension

Text visualization

So far, we have been dealing only with numeric datasets. There is a vast world of other kinds of information that visualization experts are interested in. A vast amount of text data is present in websites, books, logs, and different documents. They tend to be unstructured and not as nice-behaving as numeric datasets. Text visualization has been gaining momentum in recent days, and there are interesting and insightful techniques being developed in the visualization community. In this section, to demonstrate Mathematica's capability to handle text data, we will build a small tool from scratch to visualize the evolution of frequent words over the length of a text document.

A modified word cloud

We have all seen the word cloud. The word cloud is a simple concept that points out the underlying theme words in a document just by counting the frequency of occurrence for each particular word and rendering the words in a diagram with the font size being proportional to the frequency. Often, this gives a qualitatively accurate portrayal of the document's theme and main concepts.

What the word cloud essentially misses out is the *time* information. It is possible that a document has a word occurring very frequently at the beginning of the document, and is not present at all in the other sections. Due to its initial frequency, it may be rendered with the largest font. However, this may not be the dominant theme of the document. A possible way to get around this problem is to divide the document into smaller pieces and compute the word count per piece. In this way, we can track the words that show up in the word cloud by plotting a graph of their counts in each piece. Figure 4.12 shows the visualization we are going to code. The document that we will be using for our demo is the United Nations' human rights statement, present in the example data repository:

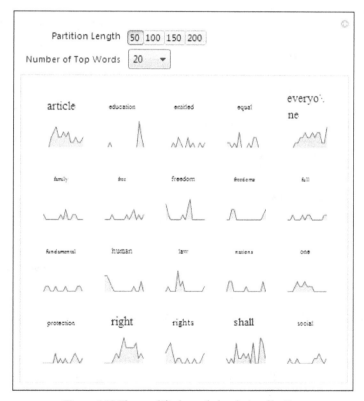

Figure 4.12 The modified word cloud visualization

In our modified word cloud, the most frequent words are laid out in alphabetical order, and are sized according to their total counts. A partition length option decides the number of words present in each piece of the document (basically, it decides the smoothness of the curves), and there is an option to view more top words by selecting the number of top words present in the drop-down list. Note how we can easily track the themes over the length of the document in our visualization. For example, *education* (the second word in the cloud) looks like a dominant theme, but is only mentioned at the beginning and at the end, whereas *everyone* and *right* occur throughout the document.

Cleaning the data

Throughout the book, we have concentrated on nicely structured datasets. In reality, the first task a data visualizer takes on is cleaning a raw dataset to give it some structure. There can be redundant columns and rows, missing values, strange file formats, and so on. The first task is usually parsing the dataset to look for anomalies, and restructuring it so that it is easier to apply algorithms.

In this project, we will take a stab at such cleaning. This will be done as an exercise to make ourselves more confident in using Mathematica to perform data cleaning. A text document usually has some frequent words (prepositions, parts of speech, and so on) that have nothing to do with the theme of a document. In a standard natural language-processing project, the first job is to get rid of these words, which are known as "stop words." In the data folder of this chapter, code repository, we have provided a text file that contains a list of such stop words. We will load this file and remove any word in the UN statement that is found in the stop words list. Other than stop words, we have punctuation and other unwanted symbols that we do not want to count. We will also remove those from the document.

The basic algorithm

First, we will load the UN human rights document and convert all words to lowercase to avoid any disambiguation that may arise from capitalization. Next, we will split the document into a list of words based on whitespace, commas, periods, and some other punctuation marks. Using the stop words list, we will filter out the stop words from this accumulated word list. We will also filter out numbers and empty strings. Next, we will count the occurrence of each word in the filtered word list, sort the words according to the total count, and choose a number of top words (defined by the user).

Once we have the top words list, we will partition the document by a user-defined number, and scan for these top words in each partition. Based on their count in each partition, we will visualize the count plot for each word, along with the word itself.

Although this may seem like a fairly long list of tasks, Mathematica makes our life easy, and we will not have to write a lot of code!

Code and explanation

We will divide and explain the code in different chunks based on different tasks. Most of the processes are inside the `Manipulate` function:

```
(* Interactive word evolution visualization in a text document *)
SetDirectory[ NotebookDirectory[ ] ]
tdat = StringSplit[ ToLowerCase[ ExampleData[ {"Text","UNHumanRightsE
nglish"}] ],
 {",","  ",";",".","--",":","]","[","(",")"} ];
stopwords = StringSplit[ Import[ "data/stop-words.txt" ], "\n"];
```

In the initialization, we load the document using the `ExampleData` function, pass the output to a lower case function, and split the resulting string using the function `StringSplit`. The `StringSplit` function takes in a string as its first argument and splits it using the list of delimiters provided as a list in the second argument. At the end of the process, we have `tdat` that contains a list of words without any punctuation. We then load and store the stop words in `stopword`. Next, let's start writing our `Manipulate` function:

```
Manipulate[
(* get rid of stop words from tdat *)
(* divide the document into chunks of words *)
tdat2 = Select[ tdat, !MemberQ[stopwords, #] &];
tdat2 = Select[ tdat2, # !="" &];
tdat2 = Select[ tdat2, !NumberQ[ ToExpression[#] ] &];
tdat2 = Partition[ tdat2, partitionlength];
wordscore = SortBy[ Tally[ Flatten[ tdat2 ] ], #[[2]] &];
(* scale wordscore to [0, 1] *)
maxcount = Max[ wordscore[[;;, 2]] ];
wordscore = Table[ { wordscore[[i,1]],
 wordscore[[i,2]]*(1.0/maxcount) }, {i,1,Length[wordscore]} ];
```

We start with a fresh list `tdat2`, and pass it through several filters using the `Select` function. First, all the elements of `tdat` that are not members of the `stopwords` list are filtered and returned to `tdat2`. The `MemberQ` function checks whether the second argument occurs in the list passed as the first argument.

Next, we check whether there are any empty strings ("") in tdat2, and select only the elements that are not. Then, using the NumberQ function, we throw away any number that is present in the list. This is all there is to data cleaning, really. At this stage, we have a list of words that are stored in tdat2 in the same sequence they occur in the document, with only the stop words and punctuation removed. Now, using the Partition function, we divide this words list into sublists of words. The variable partitionlength is the Manipulate function's own control variable.

Now, we need to find the count for each of the words throughout the document, and sort them so we can pick the top words. First, we use Tally to find the word count in tdat2, and sort the results according to the second column of the result from Tally. Remember that the elements from the output of Tally looks like: {{rights, 29}, {everyone, 23}, ...} and a bit more. The SortBy function sorts a list according to a given ordering. In this case, we simply ask SortBy to use the second column (the counts) from the output of Tally as a guide for sorting.

For convenience, we scale all the word scores in the wordscore list by dividing every count number by the maximum count. Using the Max function, we find the maximum word count in wordscore, and modify the wordscore list using Table, putting the word as the first element and scaled score as the second element in each sublist. The following piece of code takes the top words and counts them in each individual partition:

```
(* Choose the top ranked words and find their evolution *)
topwords = wordscore[[ Length[wordscore] - numwords - 1 ;;
Length[wordscore]] ];
topwords = SortBy[ topwords, #[[1]] &];
score = Table[
 currword = topwords[[i, 1]];
 Count[ tdat2[[j]], currword ],
{i,1,Length[topwords]}, {j,1,Length[tdat2]} ];
peakcount = Max[ Flatten[ score ] ];
```

Here, numwords is a control variable in Manipulate, so the user can select its value (we will see the declaration of the control variables at the end of the Manipulate section). Since wordscore is sorted in ascending order, we choose the last numwords number of elements from the list wordscore, and put them in the list topwords. Next, using a Table and a Count function (which simply counts the number of times a given element occurs in a list), we find the individual count for each word in each partition. The Table loops through topwords and tdat2 in a nested fashion, and counts the number of times currword occurs in tdat2[[j]].

Now, we have the count per segment of the document for all the top words, so we can now proceed to build our visualization using the following code:

```
(* build a table of listplot graphics elements *)
ncols = 5;
nrows = numwords / ncols;
visgrid = Table[
 currelement = ncols * (i - 1) + j;
 lstplot = ListPlot[ score[[ currelement ]], Joined->True, Mesh-
>None, PlotRange->{0, peakcount}, Filling->Bottom, Axes->False,
ImageSize->50];
 GraphicsColumn[ { Text[ Style[ topwords[[ currelement, 1 ]], FontSize
-> topwords[[ currelement, 2 ]] * 10 + 5]], lstplot }],
 {i, 1, nrows},{j, 1, ncols}
]; (* end of Table *)
GraphicsGrid[ visgrid ],
{ {partitionlength, 50, "Partition Length"}, {50,100,150,200} },
{ {numwords, 20, "Number of Top Words"}, {20,30,40,50,60,70,80,90,100}
}
] (* end of Manipulate *)
```

In this piece of code, we have drawn a table of `ListPlot` elements. First, we decide the number of desired columns and rows to show. Then, we build a table of plots and store it in the `visgrid` list. To find the correct index of the plot data in `score`, we calculate `ncols * (i - 1) + j`, which basically recomputes the two-dimensional table index (i, j) into a single-dimensional index so that the elements of `score` can be accessed. Then, the list plot is generated and stored in `lstplot` as a graphics object. Using the `GraphicsColumn` function, we define a column of the `Graphics` objects where the first row is the word (rendered using the function `Text[ Style [ ... ] ]`, and the font size is set according to the scaled score for the particular word), and the second row is `lstplot`.

So, each element of the table is essentially a graphics column that consists of two graphics elements—the word text and the list plot. Finally, we render the table using the function `GraphicsGrid`, which expects a table of graphics elements as its argument. The control variables (`partitionlength` and `numwords`) are defined next, along with their possible values. Write the whole `Manipulate` function in a cell and evaluate the cell to render our visualization (figure 4.12). You can play with different values of partition length to see how the graph shapes are affected.

Graphs and networks

We will finish this chapter with the basics of graph and network visualization in Mathematica. This is an active area of research, and there are robust and powerful software that can render very big graphs using smart data structures and graph-rendering algorithms. Mathematica is not the best tool out there for a visualization scientist who would like to render very big graphs. However, for small- to medium-sized graphs (for example, a few thousand nodes), Mathematica provides very nice visualization functions and a lot of network analysis packages.

A graph consists of nodes (often called vertices, plural of vertex) and edges, where nodes store information for any particular data type, and edges are the relationships between the nodes. An edge connects two nodes. Edges can be directed (connect nodes one way) or undirected. Social networks are often described with graphs to denote relationship between friends and family. More interestingly, many real-world problems can be boiled down to a set of relationships between different entities, and then using graph algorithms, one can gain new insights into the problems.

A basic graph visualization

We will play with some of the graph visualization capabilities of Mathematica to get a feel on the range of possibilities available to us. The dataset used for this section is present in the example data repository. It is the somewhat famous Les Misérables character coappearance network. In the full dataset, the nodes are the novel's character names and the edges are the relationships between them. In a shorter version of the network, the character names are replaced by their serial numbers.

Representing graphs in Mathematica

To create a graph in Mathematica, we use the following syntax:

```
Graph[{e₁, e₂, …}]
```

We can also use the following syntax:

```
Graph[{v₁, v₂, …}, {e₁, e₂, …}]
```

Here, ei and vi represent the edges and vertices, respectively. Take the following code, for example:

```
Graph[{1 \[UndirectedEdge] 2, 2 \[UndirectedEdge] 3, 3 \
[UndirectedEdge] 1} ]
```

This code will yield a graph with 1 connected to 2, 2 connected to 3, and 3 connected to 1. Here, 1, 2, and 3 are numbers that are nodes in the graph. Instead of numbers, we could have strings, images, or other Mathematica objects as nodes. In Mathematica, the syntax \ [UndirectedEdge] converts to a smaller edge symbol automatically when writing the code in the notebook. Alternatively, one could use the symbols < - > to represent an undirected edge, instead of \ [UndirectedEdge].

Visualizing the Les Misérables network

In order to extract the list of vertices of a graph, we may use the function VertexList. Similarly, the EdgeList function can be used to return the edges of a graph, as shown in the following lines of code:

```
g = ExampleData[{"NetworkGraph", "LesMiserables"}, "FullGraph"]
v = VertexList[g];
e = EdgeList[g];
```

Here, we have loaded the full graph data from the example data repository and stored it in g. Here, g is represented in the same structure as the previous structure, with undirected edges between the nodes. Next, we use VertexList and EdgeList to store the vertex and edges of g in v and e. When g is loaded, Mathematica will automatically render the graph with a nice layout, and output it if the line output was not suppressed with a semicolon. The following screenshot (figure 4.13) shows one such default layout:

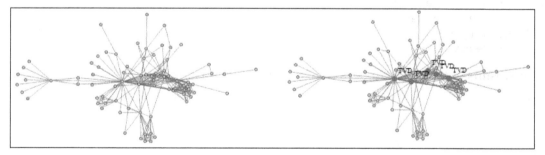

Figure 4.13 (left) The default layout of the Les Misérable graph, and (right) the vertices with the top degrees highlighted.

Highlighting centrality measures

The degree of a node refers to the number of edges that are connected to the particular node. This defines a basic measure of connectedness between vertices; it is called the DegreeCentrality. We can count the degree of each vertex in the graph using the function VertexDegree.

Figure 4.13 (right) shows the top five vertices in the graph in terms of degree. To highlight the vertices in the default layout, we write the following code:

```
top5degree = v[[ Ordering[ VertexDegree[g] ] ]] [[ -5;; ]];
HighlightGraph[ g, Labeled[ top5degree, "TVD" ], VertexSize-> Table[
top5degree[[ i ]] -> 1.2, {i,5} ] ]
```

The vertices are ordered based on the `VertexDegree` function, which returns a number for each vertex that denotes the degree of the vertex. The last five entries in the list are then chosen, which are just the top five vertices. We then use the function `HighlightGraph` to highlight the nodes of our choice. This function takes the graph g and a list of vertices to highlight under the `Labeled` function. We label each vertex with the string `"TVD"`. As an optional argument, the size of the highlighted vertices is set to 1.2 using the `VertexSize` option, to make them bigger.

Speaking of centrality measures, another interesting measure is the `BetweennessCentrality` function. For each vertex, it counts how many times the vertex is traversed while finding the shortest path between all pairs of nodes in the graph. This finds the nodes that act as a bridge between groups of nodes. Let's also highlight the top characters in the graph who act as a bridge between other characters using the following code:

```
top5bc = v[[ Ordering[ BetweennessCentrality[g] ] ]] [[ -5;; ]];
HighlightGraph[ g, Labeled[ top5bc, "TBC"], VertexSize-> Table[
top5bc[[ i ]] -> 1.2, {i,5} ] ]
(* scale the vertex sizes according to betweenness centrality *)
bc = BetweennessCentrality[g];
HighlightGraph[ g, VertexList[g], VertexSize-> Thread[ VertexList[g]
-> Rescale[bc] ] ]
```

The results of the code can be seen in the following screenshot:

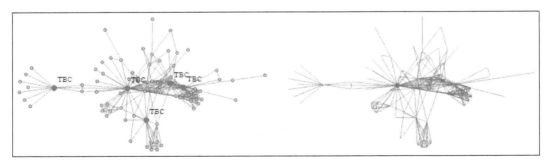

Figure 4.14 (left) The top five vertices in terms of betweenness centrality,
(right) all vertices scaled according to the measure

Similar to the case of degree centrality, we calculate the top five vertices in terms of betweenness centrality and produce a highlighted graph at first. Note how the characters that act as a bridge between groups of people are highlighted in the graph. Next, we highlight and scale the vertices according to their betweenness score. To do this, we store all scores in `bc`, and call `HighlightGraph` with `VertexSize` set according to the scores. The `Thread` function takes each element of `VertexList[g]` and `Rescale[bc]` and pairs them together.

Other graph layouts

Often, 2D graph layouts are congested. Mathematica provides a suite of layout options to arrange the nodes in the diagram in different ways. Figure 4.15 shows two other layouts. Radial layout attempts to arrange the vertices hierarchically according to their degree, and spring embedding shows how the graph will look like if the edges were to act as springs in a mass spring simulation. Right-clicking on the current graph layout will show a menu for styling the graph. Under the Graph Layout section, we will find the options for other layouts.

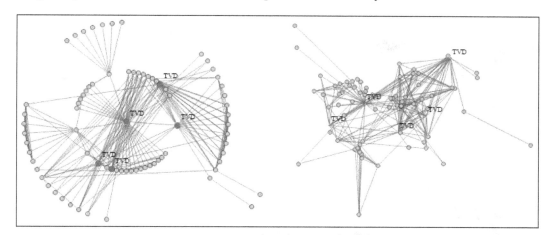

Figure 4.15 (left) The radial layout and (right) the spring-embedding layout

Layout algorithms are researched extensively in the visualization community. They often involve force-based simulations (where nodes exert force on each other) and shape-packing algorithms from computational geometry and other approaches.

3D layouts

We can take a step further and render the graph in 3D using the `GraphPlot3D` command. This provides a better way to view the node relationships from different angles:

```
GraphPlot3D[ g, VertexLabeling->True, EdgeRenderingFunction-> (
{LightBlue, Cylinder[#1, 0.03]} &), VertexRenderingFunction-> (
{EdgeForm[Black], LightGreen, Sphere[#1, 0.2], Black, Text[ #2, #1]}
&), Lighting->"Neutral"]
```

The `GraphPlot3D` function simply takes in `g` and plots it in 3D. We have provided our custom edge-rendering and vertex-rendering functions. The edge-rendering function dictates `GraphPlot3D` to render thin cylinders (0.03 units radius) of light blue color, and the vertex-rendering function defines the nodes as small green spheres of radius 0.2 units. Figure 4.16 shows the result from different angles:

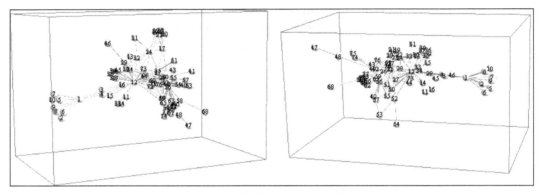

Figure 4.16 A 3D graph layout

Chord diagrams

Even though the graph layout algorithms are useful, I promised that we would employ interactivity in our visualization prototypes whenever there is a need. A simple way to arrange our graph is to put the nodes around the perimeter of a circle, and show the connections between them using curves. The basic visualization behind this notion is known as a chord diagram. We will finish the chapter with an interactive chord diagram that gives a whole new dimension to the exploration of relationships in a graph.

The following figure 4.17 shows a chord diagram of the characters of Les Misérables:

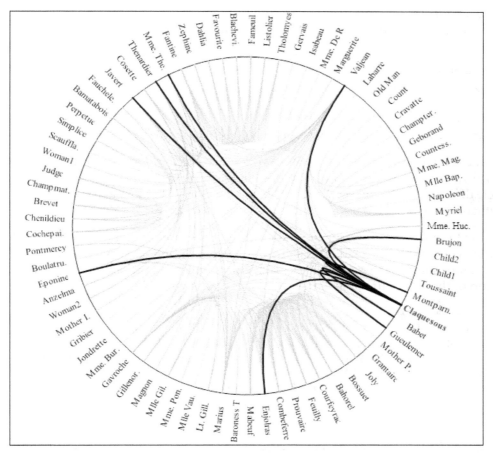

Figure 4.17 An interactive chord diagram. Entities and their relations can be highlighted
when the mouse pointer hovers over them

The chord diagram is useful for visualizing relationships in a macro and micro scale.
The overall diagram gives a sense of the density and the flow of relationships between
the nodes by bundling groups of edges together. Putting the mouse pointer over
each name gives us a particular character's relationships. In figure 4.17, **Claquesous**
is highlighted.

Code and explanation

The code mostly involves playing around with the geometry of the text locations and curve placement. We start off by loading the data and defining some parameters:

```
g = ExampleData[{"NetworkGraph","LesMiserables"},"FullGraph"]
v = VertexList[g]
e = EdgeList[g];
r = 10;
tsep = 1.0;
ang = 2Pi / Length[v] + 0.0;
```

Here, r is the radius of the circle within which the edges reside. tsep is the separation between the text and the perimeter of the circle. ang is the unit angle — it is the angle difference between each node. The value 0.0 is added to make sure that the Mathematica expression assigns a numeric value to ang.

The next piece of code creates the static curves. Note that the diagram consists of two sets of curves. The static and semi-transparent light blue curves represent all the relationships, whereas the thick black curves are dynamic, and are rendered on top of the static curves when the mouse is over a name.

```
gelt2 = Table[
 vind1 = Position[ v, e[[i,1]] ] [[1,1]];
 vind2 = Position[ v, e[[i,2]] ] [[1,1]];
 { Opacity[0.5], RGBColor[0.6,0.729,1], BSplineCurve[{ {(r-0.5) * Cos[
ang*vind1 ], (r-0.5) * Sin[ ang*vind1 ] }, {0,0}, {(r-0.5) * Cos[
ang*vind2 ], (r-0.5) * Sin[ ang*vind2 ]} }]
 },
{i,1,Length[e]}];
```

Here, we create a table of BSplineCurve graphics objects. Bezier splines (B-splines) are smooth curves that can be generated using a set of control points. Our goal is to draw a curve for each edge. An edge connects two nodes, so we draw a curve from one node's coordinates to the next node's coordinates. To do this, we loop through the edge list e and find the positions of the nodes of each edge inside the vertex list v, storing the indices in vind1 and vind2. Next, the table element is defined within the curly brackets. It is the graphics description for the B-Spline curve. We set the opacity to 0.5, and define a custom light blue color for each curve. The BSplineCurve takes in a list of control points and returns a graphics object that stores the description of the curve.

The curve is defined by three points. From simple trigonometry, we know that given the polar coordinate (r and angle ang*vind1), we can find the corresponding (x, y) coordinate from (r * cos(ang*vind1), r * sin(ang*vind1)). Based on the formula, we define three control points, two for the positions of the vertices, and one at the center (0, 0). The extra center coordinate gives us the bent curves shown in figure 4.17. Next, we write the following code for the dynamic curves:

```
gdyn = Table[
 cv = v[[j]];
 tempe = EdgeList[g, cv \[UndirectedEdge] _];
 rot = (ang*j > Pi/2) && (ang*j < 3*Pi/2);

 Mouseover[
 (* if mouse not on top *)
 (* render the character name *)
 Rotate[ Text[ Style[
  (* Limit the character name to 8 characters only *)
  If[ StringLength[cv]>8, StringTake[cv,8] <> ".", cv], Medium],
  {(r+tsep) * Cos[ang*j], (r+tsep) * Sin[ang*j] }], If[rot, ang*j-Pi,
ang*j] ],

 { (* if mouse on top *)
 (* render the character name *)
 Rotate[ Text[ Style[ cv, Medium, Blue, Bold], {(r+tsep) *
Cos[ang*j],(r+tsep) * Sin[ang*j]} ], If[rot, ang*j-Pi, ang*j]
 ],
 (* render thick bsplines curves *)
 Table[
  vind1 = Position[v, tempe[[i,1]] ] [[1,1]];
  vind2 = Position[v, tempe[[i,2]] ] [[1,1]];
  {
   Thick, BSplineCurve[{ {(r-0.5) * Cos[ang*vind1],(r-0.5)*
Sin[ang*vind1]}, {0,0}, {(r-0.5) * Cos[ang*vind2], (r-0.5)*
Sin[ang*vind2]} }]
  },
  {i,1,Length[tempe]}] (* end of thick b-spline table *)

 } (* end of Mouseover second argument *)
 ], (* end of Mouseover *)

{j,1,Length[v]}]; (* end of gdyn table *)
```

Even though this is quite a bit of code, it is not quite complex. We would like to create a table of Mouseover elements that we will eventually pass on to a Graphics function. Inside the Mouseover function, we have two arguments. The first argument is applicable when the mouse is not on top of the *j*th character name, in which case we simply render the character name. The second argument defines what to draw when the mouse is over the *j*th character name. The loop j goes over the vertex list.

tempe finds the edges that are connected to the current node, cv. The EdgeList function, in this case, looks for the pattern cv \[UndirectedEdge] _ in g, where _ is a placeholder to denote any vertex. Then, we define a Boolean variable rot, which determines whether the current vertex angle falls within a certain range. Next, we enter the Mouseover argument.

If the mouse is not on top of the *j*th vertex, then we only render the character names. The text is trimmed using StringTake, and then styled and rotated. It is placed at a distance r + tsep from the center. For the rotation, we use the condition If[rot, ang*j-Pi, ang*j]. This determines whether to flip the names around if they are within a certain range of angles.

If the mouse is on top of the name, we render the name along with all the B-spline curves that correspond to the edges in tempe. The character name placement code is the same as before, except that the style is changed to bold and blue. For the B-spline curves, we essentially use the same code used to create gelt2, but this time, we style the curves to be black and thicker, and the table loops through all of tempe.

Finally, in the following code, we use the Graphics function to combine these elements along with a circle:

```
Graphics[{Circle[ {0,0}, r - 0.5], gelt2, gdyn}]
```

Evaluating the cells (the code is in the Chapter4 code folder) will give us the dynamic chord diagram.

Tweaking the visualization

We can order the nodes according to the rank of their degree. This changes the structure of the chord diagram. In general, bundles of edges that flow from one region within the circle to another region reveal relationship patterns in the graph that would otherwise be hard to see using the graph layouts available to us.

In order to change the vertex ordering, we can store the vertices in v (at the beginning of the code) sorted according to the vertex degrees:

```
v = VertexList[g] [[ Ordering[ VertexDegree[g] ] ]]
```

The output based on the original ordering of the vertices is shown in the following figure:

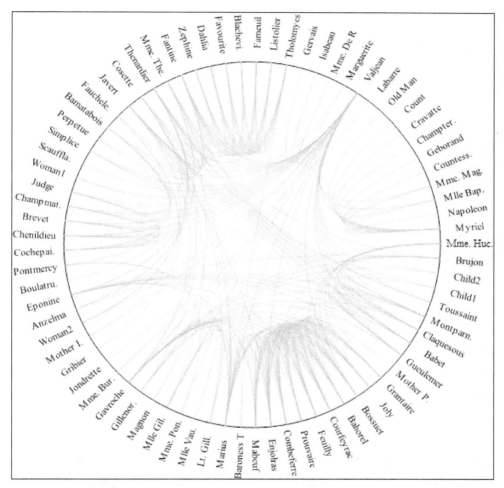

Figure 4.18 The chord structure based on natural ordering of the vertices in the dataset

Figures 4.18 and 4.19 show the comparison between the two vertex-ordering methods:

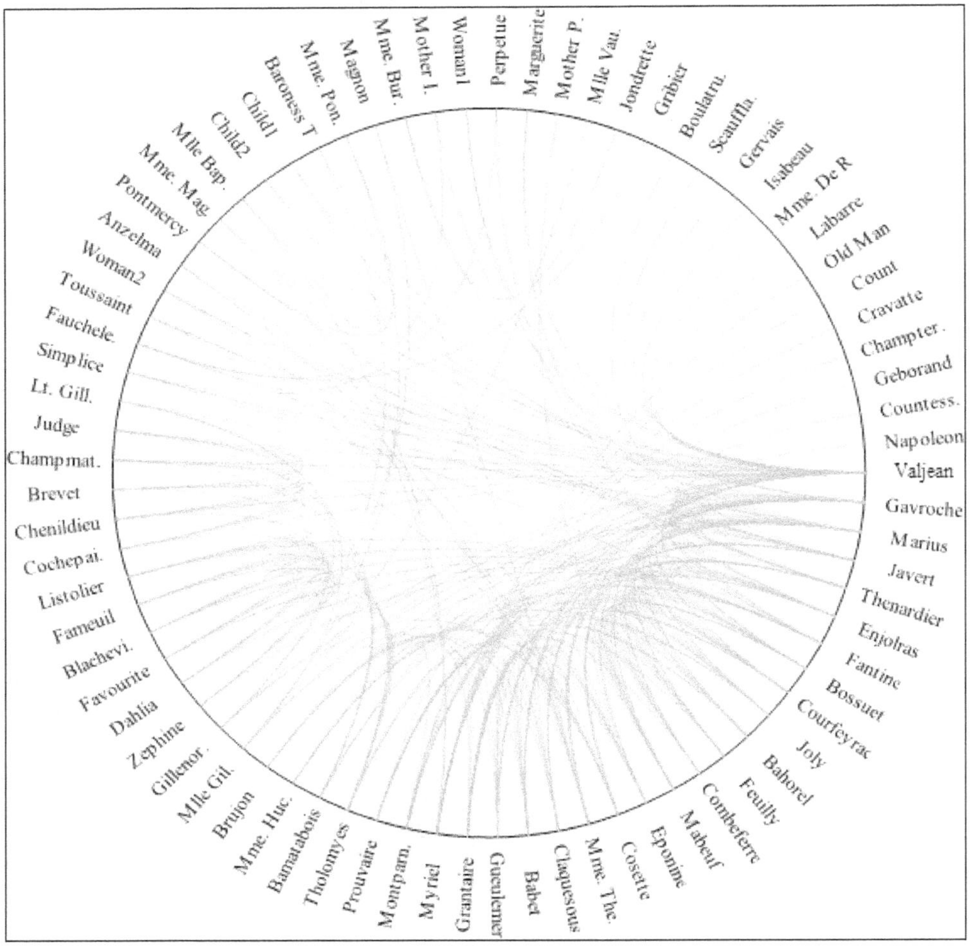

Figure 4.19 The chord structure after the vertices are ordered based on degree

Further reading

The literature on information visualization is quite broad. A complete reference of the statistical plots in Mathematica can be found in the documentation along with some tutorials on the plot functions that were not covered here. For those interested in an in-depth analysis of graph drawing and layout algorithms, *Handbook of Graph Drawing and Visualization*, by *Roberto Tamassia*, a computer science professor at Brown University, published by CRC Press, can prove to be useful.

Summary

In this chapter, we have demonstrated some capabilities of Mathematica to create interactive information-visualization prototypes. Starting with the statistical plot functions, we have eventually moved on to text and graph data. We have demonstrated a possible visualization technique to view high-dimensional data. Then, we have created our own word cloud tool that reveals the frequency evolution of words over the length of a document. Some of Mathematica's graph data visualization capabilities are demonstrated in the *Graphs and networks* section. Finally, we have developed an interactive chord diagram tool to view the character relationships in the novel Les Misérables. In the next chapter, we will write a map visualization tool and discuss some essential aesthetic matters that every data visualization scientist should know.

5
Maps and Aesthetics

In *Chapter 3, Time Series and Scientific Visualization* and *Chapter 4, Statistical and Information Visualization*, we learned how to use Mathematica to create visualization prototypes. We saw how Mathematica's Graphics language and interactivity functions — coupled with its plotting packages — allow us to create visualization tools of our design and choice. The last chapter of the book will be much shorter than the others. We will learn to create map visualizations, and briefly discuss how colors, interactivity, and design choices affect maps and other visualizations.

Map visualization

In Mathematica 10, Wolfram Research introduced an extended version of the Graphics package; it is called the GeoGraphics package. It provides several useful functions to visualize maps and cartographic data. However, there is a limitation in the usage of this package as of now. Some of the data and map loaders in the new geological functions require Internet connectivity and Wolfram | Alpha API calls. The number of API calls is usually restricted to a fairly small number per month. This can be a limiting factor if you are trying to work on a data-intensive project.

In this chapter, we will see some examples of using the GeoGraphics package. Then, just like the other chapters in this book, we will develop our very own interactive map visualization code from scratch, using raw (and offline) datasets. This gives us the ability to produce similar visualizations such as GeoGraphics, but with more interactivity and control over our data.

The GeoGraphics package

The basic syntax for the package is the as follows:

```
GeoGraphics[primitives, options]
```

In the `primitives` argument, we can enter several new geographic primitives introduced in Version 10, along with the standard geometry primitives, such as color and polygon forms. Some of these new geographic primitives are as follows:

- `GeoPosition[{lat,long}]`: This is used to represent a point in latitude and longitude
- `GeoMarker[]`: This represents the current location of the computer
- `GeoRange`: This is an option argument in `GeoGraphics` that represents a bounding circle radius around a center coordinate
- `GeoDisk[location, r]`: This represents a disk of radius r around the geographic center location
- `GeoPath[{loc1, loc2, ...}, pathtype]`: This represents a list of points {loc1, loc2, ...} that indicate a path or track in the `pathtype` geographic coordinate system

There are several other geographic primitives, but for our examples, these are sufficient. The preceding list will not make much sense until we see them in action. Here are some examples that demonstrate the ease of using the `GeoGraphics` package.

A map of our current location

To start things off, we will create a map of our current location:

```
GeoGraphics[GeoMarker[], GeoRange -> Quantity[4,"Miles"]]
```

Using the `GeoMarker` primitive, we ask for a map of our current location, setting the `GeoRange` option to 4 miles. `Quantity[magnitude, unit]` is a function that represents a scalar value, and it's used here to represent a value for `GeoRange`. Figure 5.1 shows the result.

Note that `GeoMarker` might take a two-dimensional point as its argument. In this case, our code will display a map with a radius of 4 miles centering around the point of interest. The preceding code calls the Wolfram | Alpha API, so Internet connectivity is required.

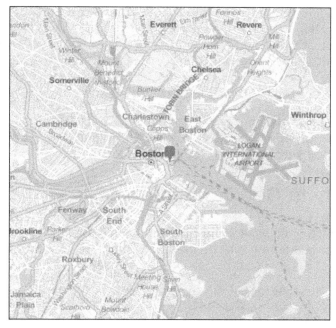

Figure 5.1 A map of the area around the current location of the computer

Plotting a path on the map

The following code plots a path in a specific geographical coordinate system:

```
locations={ GeoPosition[{-71,42}], GeoPosition[{-83,107}] };
GeoGraphics[{Red, GeoDisk[locations[[1]],Quantity[100,"Kilom
eter"]], GeoDisk[locations[[2]],Quantity[100,"Kilometer"]],
GeoPath[locations,"Geodesic"]}, GeoRange->"Country", GeoProjection-
>"Mercator"]
```

Figure 5.2 displays the result:

Figure 5.2 Plotting a path in the Mercator projection system

First, we define a pair of points using the GeoPosition primitive function. Then, GeoGraphics is called to render the map with two disks. The disks use the locations we defined earlier, and are each 100 km in radius. The GeoGraphics primitive GeoPath represents a line in the Geodesic projection system. GeoRange is used to define a particular range to render the map. The map is rendered using the Mercator projection system (a cylindrical map projection system used in geological science).

Note the change in the disk radius along the path. This is due to the particular projection system we chose to render the map. The Mercator projection system exaggerates areas as we go farther from the equator.

Interactivity in GeoGraphics

We can use ToolTip and similar context-aware functions to make GeoGraphics more interactive. The following is adapted from one of the example codes in the Mathematica documentation. We use the BridgeData function to find and display all the bridges in the city of Cambridge in Massachusetts:

```
bd = BridgeData[ GeoNearest["Bridge", Entity["City",{"Cambridge",
"Massachusetts","UnitedStates"}], {All,Quantity[5,"Kilometer"]}],
{"Position","Image"}];

GeoGraphics[{Blue,PointSize[.03],Tooltip[Point[#1],#2] & @@@ bd}]
```

Figure 5.3 shows the output when hovering the mouse pointer over one of the points:

Figure 5.3 Rendering images of bridges as a tooltip within GeoGraphics

The `BridgeData` function returns data on bridges in a particular area defined by its parameters. `GeoNearest[entity type, location]` returns a geographic entity based on the location provided. Here, we define a general broad location using the geographical function `Entity["City", {"Cambridge", "Massachusetts", "UnitedS tates"}]`, where `Cambridge` is the city, located in the state of `Massachusetts`, within the country of `UnitedStates`. We also ask `GeoNearest` to search within a 5km radius. Finally, we only extract the `Position` and `Image` fields from `BridgeData`.

Once we have the position and image tuple for each bridge, we map the `ToolTip` function to each of these tuples using the `@@@` operator, which is a shortcut to apply a function on every element in a list. This happens within `GeoGraphics`, which renders all the tooltips together, along with a blue dot at each location of the bridge on the map.

There are several interesting examples in the documentation that show how to use `GeoGraphics` in various ways. However, as mentioned at the beginning of the chapter, we are limited by the restricted Wolfram | Alpha API calls. It is better to understand the nuts and bolts of a map visualization system to acquire more control over our data and analysis pipeline. The next section demonstrates the skeleton of a map visualization engine in Mathematica.

Anatomy of a map visualization engine

The standard map visualization scenario is explained here. Usually, we are given a shape-description file that has the polygon information for a particular area's map. These files can be downloaded for free from an open source map repository such as **OpenStreetMap**. We will want to load the file, acquire the polygon information from the data, and store it as a list of polygons, so we can use `Graphics` to render the polygons together. Now, the data that we try to visualize can come in many varieties. For simplicity, we can assume that we have numeric datasets associated with the polygons.

For example, we might want to visualize the annual expenditure for the lower 48 states of the US. To create the map, we require a shape description file for the US. The file will have the polygon information for each state's geographic shape. We will also want access to the actual expenditure values, and we will want to fill each polygon with a color based on the expenditure for each state.

In the `data` folder of the `Chapter5` code bundle folder, there is a shape-description file (`.shp` format) named `usa_state_shapefile.shp`. Along with the shape file, we have 10 CSV files, `usgs_state_2001.csv`, ..., `usgs_state_2010.csv`, which contain the state name and expenditure values from 2001 to 2010. Each row contains a state's name, followed by the expenditure information in the second column. There are other information columns too, and the interested reader can change the code to visualize the other columns of data. The rows are sorted according to the alphabetical ordering of the states. We will use these datasets to create a map visualization.

The visual interface

We essentially have a time series for each state. We will like to see how the state's expenses vary from 2001 to 2010. To visualize this, we will fill each polygon with a color. In this case, we will demonstrate how we can build our own simple color map using a `Graphics` primitive. The following screenshot shows the interface we are going to build:

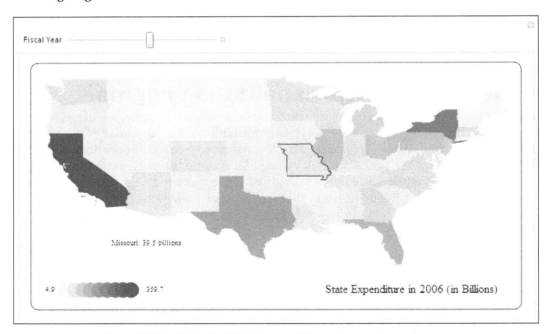

Figure 5.4 Visualizing the US state expenditure using a custom color map

The **Fiscal Year** slider will change the year from 2001 to 2010, so we can see the transition of colors between different states as years change. On the bottom left, we show our custom color map, which is a uniform blending from light brown to blue. The visualization is interactive, so each state polygon will have a mouse-over behavior that displays a text stating the individual state's expenses. In figure 5.4, the mouse pointer is over the Missouri state's polygon, so it is highlighted with a black boundary, and a small text below the map shows the annual spending of Missouri.

We will use the `Manipulate` function to create the interface, within which we will render a `Graphics` object that holds all the polygons and text information.

Code and explanation

We start by loading the `.shp` and `.csv` files:

```
SetDirectory[ NotebookDirectory[] ]
shpdat = Import["data/usa_state_shapefile.shp", "Data"]
names = shpdat[[1, 4, 2, 2, 2]];
polys = "Geometry" /. shpdat[[1]]
filenames = Table["data/usgs_state_" <> ToString[i] <> ".csv", {i,
2001, 2010}]
yeardats = Map[Import, filenames];
yeardats = Table[Select[yeardats[[i]], Length[#] == 11 &], {i, 1,
10}];
```

`shpdat` loads the `Data` property of the shape file. Other than this property, the file contains many other additional attributes, such as names of the states, header information, and so on. Mentioning the `Data` property to the `Import` function loads the relevant portion of the file, namely, the geometry information. Since we do need the names of the states along with the geometry, we access the relevant element in `shpdat` using `shpdat[[ 1,4,2,2,2 ]]`. This might seem a little random, and in fact, it came out of some data hacking. There are many data file formats out there, and whenever we work with something that is not commonly used, we will need to deal with the list structure returned after importing it in Mathematica. In this case, exploring the sublists one at a time (by printing them out) revealed the level at which the names were located.

Next, we extract the polygon information from the `Geometry` header of `shpdat` using the `/.` operator. This is a standard way to extract information from lists that have header information with them. `shpdat` looks like the following:

```
{{Names -> {Alabama, Alaska, …}, Geometry -> {Polygon[{…}],
Polygon[{…}], …}, …}}
```

Basically, we have lists of information that have headers (for example, Names, Geometry, and so on) associated with them. `"Geometry" /. shpdat[[1]]` returns us the list that has the Polygons element.

Then, we create a table of filenames for the `.csv` files, and load them using the `Import` function mapped to each one of the filenames. The data for each year is filtered to get rid of the header information by selecting only the rows that have 11 columns. By scrutinizing the file structure, it was found that all the relevant rows have 11 columns.

The next piece of code prepares the expenditure data:

```
spending = Table[yeardats[[i]][[2 ;;, 2]], {i, 1, 10}];
population = Table[yeardats[[i]][[2 ;;, 10]], {i, 1, 10}];
spendingscaled = Table[spending[[i]] / Max[spending[[i]]], {i, 1,
10}];
populationscaled =
  Table[population[[i]]/Max[population[[i]]], {i, 1, 10}];
```

The second column of the `.csv` files has the expenditure values for states, and the tenth column has the population. We extract these numbers as a list from `yeardats`, and scale them to lie between 0 and 1 for convenience. The matrices can be checked just by printing them in the output cell at this point. The rows are the years and the columns are the state names, and each (i, j) entry is the spending value for the ith year and the jth state, respectively. The population values are not used in the actual visualization, though replacing the `spendingscaled` list with `populationscaled` will yield a population visualization. This is left as an exercise. Next, we write the `Manipulate` function that creates the actual visualization:

```
Manipulate[
  polytable = Table[
    {Blend[{LightBrown, Blue}, spendingscaled[[year, i]]],
     EdgeForm[None],
     Mouseover[polys[[i]], {
       EdgeForm[Thin],
       polys[[i]],
       Black,
       Text[names[[i]] <> ": " <> ToString[spending[[year, i]]] <>
         " billions", {-112, 28}]
       }
     ]},
    {i, 1, Length[polys]}];
  polytable2 = Drop[Drop[polytable, {2}], {11}];
  Framed[Graphics[{Style[
      Text["State Expenditure in " <> ToString[2000 + year] <>
```

```
        " (in Billions)", {-79, 22}], FontSize -> 16],
    polytable2,
        Table[{Blend[{LightBrown, Blue}, x], Disk[{-122 + x*8, 22}]}, {x,
0, 1, 1/8}],
        Black,
        Text[Min[spending[[year]]], {-124, 22}],
        Text[Max[spending[[year]]], {-111, 22}]
        }, ImageSize -> 650], RoundingRadius -> 10]
  , {{year, 1, "Fiscal Year"}, 1, 10, 1}
  ]
```

The code is surprisingly small for all the things it actually does. Throughout the book, the readers must have noticed the elegance of Mathematica in achieving quite a lot while writing very little code. Inside the Manipulate function, we first create a list of the polygons that will be rendered using Graphics. Each element of polytable contains the styling information along with the actual polygon command.

At first, using the Blend function (the syntax is Blend[{color1, color2}, ratio], where ratio is a single number between [0, 1] (ranging between 0 and 1) that dictates what proportion of color1 should be mixed with color2), we create a custom color that lies between light brown and blue. The ratio of mixing is governed by spendingscaled[[year, i]], which we have already scaled between 0 and 1. The year variable is a control variable for Manipulate, which can be changed using the slider, and i loops over the number of elements in polys, which is the same as the number of states.

The EdgeForm[None] function is used to ask Graphics to not render the polygon boundaries. Next, Mouseover draws the bare polygon, polys[[i]], if the mouse pointer is not on top of this particular polygon, and draws it with a thin black boundary along with a text at the coordinate (-112, 28), which displays the name of the state along with the spending value. The symbol <> is a shorthand for the function StringJoin, which simply concatenates strings.

Once we are done building the polytable function, we define a second table named polytable2, which drops the second and eleventh elements in polytable. These correspond to Hawaii and Alaska (remember, we are only visualizing the lower 48 states). We are almost done with the processing now.

Next, we simply arrange all the elements in order inside the Graphics function. The text at the bottom-right is first rendered with a font size of 16. It changes the year name as we change the slider value. Next, we pass polytable2 to Graphics. This will render all the filled polygons for all states. Then, to provide a color map guidance to the viewer, we create a color map bar that shows filled disks progressing from light brown to blue. Finally, we put two texts at the left and right of the color bar we just created. These show the actual minimum and maximum values of spending for the currently selected year.

That's it! Evaluating the cells in the `MapVisualization.nb` notebook (provided in the code folder) will render the map visualization as seen in the first screenshot. Moving the slider reveals intermediate flow of government expenditure between eastern and western states, which is pretty amazing to watch.

This is the last mini project in the book. By now, we have covered all types of data that were mentioned in *Chapter 1, Visualization as a Tool to Understand Data*. We worked through various mini projects to gain a better understanding of the visualization and interactivity functions available in Mathematica. With this knowledge, you can hopefully go on writing your own code to create any data visualization prototype of your design and choice. However, we are left with an important discussion that every beginner in data visualization must know. The next section will briefly introduce you to some essential aesthetics and design issues in data visualization.

Aesthetics in visualization

Before we write even a single line of code, we should always sketch out our visualization's design. It is often true that over time, the design will keep changing, based on the nature of the data and the questions asked. This is another reason to use Mathematica to create any prototype, as it saves a lot of time.

Once we have the visualization designed and coded, our next concern should be the perceptibility of our visualization. Does it answer the question we asked? Is it discernible for the user or the audience? In order to tackle these issues, we should be careful about few things.

Choosing the right color map

We have already mentioned in *Chapter 4, Statistical and Information Visualization*, that even though the rainbow color map is widely used, it is bad. Unfortunately, many of the color maps provided by Mathematica also have the same problem, which makes the rainbow color map harmful. Our visualization is there to help the viewer understand deep inferences about the data. However, a bad color map can destroy the user experience. Here is why.

The rainbow color map is misleading

Data visualizations are there to save our time. Looking at our map visualization, one can infer right away what the low and high spending states are, along with the intermediate states. This will only be possible if there is a good color map. Let's say the range of values we want to map is between 0 and 1. A color map is considered good if it does not swing between different colors while we progress from 0 to 1. Why? The user will have a hard time understanding whether the orange color denotes a greater value than green. Figure 5.5 shows the rainbow color map provided by Mathematica:

Figure 5.5 Rainbow color map provided by Mathematica

The rainbow color map is based on the colors in the light spectrum — the VIBGYOR colors. Even if the user remembers all the colors in the spectrum (which is often not the case), it is sometimes very confusing to compare the intermediate values. It is not intuitive and poses a challenge to the user to understand the data. Mapping continuous-valued data to a rainbow color map is discouraged for this reason.

Understanding hue and luminance

Instead of the well-known RGB color space, a color can be represented using hue and luminance too. Hue refers to the actual colors, and luminance refers to the perceived brightness of the colors. For example, light blue or dark blue has the same hue, but their luminance changes. Figure 5.6 shows a sampling of Hue colors, generated using Mathematica.

Figure 5.6 A sampling of colors corresponding to minimum to maximum hue values

There are two problems with the rainbow color map. The first is that the hue changes a few times, and secondly, each time the hue changes, the luminance changes abruptly to generate the lighter to darker shades.

Some better color maps

As always, we will like to have a nice transition in our color map so that it is obvious to the user. There are several simple solutions. Figure 5.7 shows the concept of two simple color maps that can remedy the situation. One of them has already been used in map visualization.

Figure 5.7 (left) DeepSeaColors color map in Mathematica, and (right) custom color map (sampled) blending two hues

One way to generate a better color map is to use the same hue and vary the luminance. Throughout the book, we used the **GrayTones** color map in several visualizations, which varies the color from dark gray to light gray smoothly. Figure 5.7 (left) shows the **DeepSeaColors** color map in Mathematica. It transitions between dark to lighter blue. These color maps are examples of keeping the same hue and varying the luminance.

If we wish to change the hue in our color map, then it is better to stick to two hues only and vary the luminance between them uniformly. Figure 5.7 (right) shows the color map we used in the map visualization. There are two hues: brown and blue, but the luminance changes smoothly.

There are other complex ways to create color maps, but they require a knowledge of color theory. The readers should definitely check the **ColorBrewer** website online, which provides a database of good color maps that can be readily used in visualizations.

Designing the right interface

The 7-year-old son of one of my professors once asked him about the meaning of visualization. After he explained what data visualization means (in the simplest form possible), the professor's son replied, "Oh! So, it is like you design ways to see information, and then spend your time explaining to others how to make sense of the design itself!"

He basically figured out the problems with many data visualization interface designs right away. A complicated interface that has a steep learning curve defeats the purpose of data visualization. The visual signatures that we typically use (for example, plots, chord diagrams, parallel coordinates, and so on) should also be simple enough to convey the right amount of information.

When designing new visual signatures for new types of dataset, we should remember that visualization is essentially a coding system. It is a way to encode a lot of information in a small space. The power and beauty of it comes with the potential danger of misunderstanding if we are not careful about our design. It makes sense to design new signatures and/or interfaces if the new visualization system has the following properties:

- Ability to generate more insights once the data is visualized
- Two distinct datasets do not translate to the same visualization, or, there are well-defined rules that do not produce conflicts when it comes to transcribing the visual inference back to the real-world domain
- Ease of transcription between the visualization and the real-world inference back and forth
- Ability to compress information
- Reusability of the system for similar datasets

These are not golden rules that one has to abide by, but they raise the right questions that we should be asking when critiquing our own designs.

In general, it is better to use less buttons, controls, sliders, and so on. The visualization should not be too small or too big (so the user has to scroll around to view it). Where possible, it should be made interactive. Finally, user feedback is very important when designing visualizations. Before deploying our system, we should always test it with some users.

Deploying Mathematica visualizations

There are several ways in which we can deploy our visualizations and share them with people. We can save our Mathematica notebooks in the CDF format. Mathematica provides a free CDF player that can be downloaded to view Mathematica code and visualizations interactively. To deploy the system in your websites, you can subscribe to the **webMathematica** interface. Starting from Version 10, Mathematica will have an online interface that you can buy. The Wolfram Demonstrations site also provides a way to host our notebooks online. Details of preparing a notebook to upload in this site can be found in the documentation.

Looking forward

Within the short span of this book, we have covered a whole bunch of techniques that should make us confident about working with different kinds of data and visualizing them in Mathematica. We explored the capabilities of Mathematica for data visualization, and now it is time to start building some of your own visualizations too.

In order to tackle big datasets, you will need to know how to use Hadoop, CUDA, or MPI with Mathematica. This is not in the scope of the book, but there are books and tutorials available online that can get you started.

Mathematica is a good tool for creating data visualizations, but there are other widely used tools too. VTK, Processing, and D3.js are a few libraries that you might want to check out. Though they do not provide a single workspace to do the analysis and visualization together (as Mathematica does), they are well known and worth learning.

Good luck with your exciting endeavors in the world of data visualization!

Further reading

To understand the harmful implications of the rainbow color map, the interested reader can take a look at the academic paper *Rainbow Color Map (Still) Considered Harmful, Borland and Taylor, IEEE Journal of Computer Graphics and Applications (Vol. 27, Issue 2)*. There are several websites that provide very useful resources for aesthetics in data visualization. The eagereyes.org website has a set of nice articles on issues ranging over design, aesthetics, and colors.

Summary

In this (short) chapter, we learned how to use the GeoGraphics package, and how we can use a .shp file to create interactive map visualizations. We also learned about color maps, what kind of color maps can be harmful, and what kind is useful. Other than colors, we briefly talked about the principles of interface design. Finally, different ways to deploy our visualizations were mentioned.

Index

Symbols

2D graph layouts 105
3D layouts 106
3D point plots 43, 44

A

aesthetics, visualization
  about 124
  color maps 126
  hue 125
  luminance 125
  rainbow color map 125
  right color map, selecting 124
  right interface, designing 126, 127
append function 29
AxesOrigin property 37

B

BarLegend 41
basic algorithm 98
BubbleChart 87, 88

C

cartographic data 15
centrality measures
  highlighting 103-105
ChartLabels option 86
charts 82
ChartStyle option 86
chord diagrams
  about 106, 107
  code 108
  explanation 108-110

visualizations, tweaking 110-112
ColorBrewer 126
ColorFunction property 44
color maps, aesthetics visualization
  DeepSeaColors color map 126
  GrayTones color map 126
  hue 125
  luminance 125
  rainbow color map 125
  selecting 124
conditionals 32-34
core languages 21, 34
counterfeit clusters
  visualizing 90, 91
crit 30
CSV (comma-separated values) 35
current location, GeoGraphics package
  map 116

D

data
  importing 34
  importing, into Mathematica 34
dataset
  loading 35, 36
datasets, types
  about 11
  cartographic data 15
  graphs 14
  scalar field 12, 13
  table 12
  text 15
  time series 14
data structures 21
data, visualization 94

data, word cloud
  cleaning 98
DateListPlot function 58, 59
DeepSeaColors color map 126
DegreeCentrality 103
DensityHistogram 80

E

elements
  accessing, from list 27-29
EvenQ function 31

F

features, Mathematica 16
Filling property 37
financial data, visualization
  about 57, 58
  DateListPlot function 58, 59
  graphics 61
  interactivity, adding 60-64
  show 62
flatten function 30
functions
  about 32
  declaring 32, 33
  using 32, 33

G

gauges 81
genuine clusters
  visualizing 90-92
GeoGraphics package
  about 116
  current location, map 116
  GeoDisk[location, r] primitive 116
  GeoMarker[] primitive 116
  GeoPath[{loc1, loc2, ...}, pathtype]
     primitive 116
  GeoPosition[{lat,long}] primitive 116
  GeoRange primitive 116
  interactivity 118, 119
  path, plotting on map 117, 118
  primitives 116
graphics 61
graphs 14, 102

graph, visualization
  2D graph layouts 105
  3D layouts 106
  about 102
  centrality measures, highlighting 103-105
  creating 102, 103
  Les Misérables network, visualizing 103
GrayTones color map 91, 126

H

harmful implications, rainbow color map
  reference 128
high-dimensional data
  about 89
  counterfeit clusters, visualizing 90, 91
  genuine clusters, visualizing 90, 91
  information, projecting to
    low dimensions 90
  misleading color map, selecting 95
  similarity maps 89
  similarity maps, for datasets 92-94
  wrong distance metric, employing 94, 95
Histogram 80-84
Histogram3D 80, 85
HSB (Hue, Saturation, and Brightness) 55
hue 125

I

information, visualization 79
interactivity
  adding 60-64, 73, 74
Internet activity
  simulating 52, 53
isocontours
  about 64-67
  plot, preparing 72, 73
isosurface plot 74, 75

L

LabellingFunction property 86
Layout algorithms 105
legend, types
  about 41
  BarLegend 41
  LineLegend 41

PointLegend 41
SwatchLegend 41
length function 29
Les Misérables network
visualizing 103
LineLegend 41
ListPlot 36-38
lists
about 22
creating, programmatically 24, 25
elements, accessing from 27-29
nested lists 23
set operations, applying 29-31
log plots 44-46
low dimensions
information, projecting to 90
luminance 125

M

Manipulate function 73
map, GeoGraphics package
of current location 116
path, plotting 117, 118
map, visualization
about 115
anatomy 119
code 121
explanation 121-124
GeoGraphics package 116
visual interface 120, 121
Mathematica
about 15
data, importing into 34
features 16
Mathematica Journal
about 46
URL 46
Mathematica notebook essentials
about 17
cell formatting 18
cells, creating 17, 18
cells, evaluating 18
cells, selecting 17, 18
commenting, in cell text 19
evaluation of cell, aborting 19
output, suppressing from cell 18

matrices 23, 24
MatrixForm function 23
meters 81
miscellaneous functions 81
misleading color map
selecting 95
Module 33
molecular visualization 64
multiple elements
table elements with 27
table entries with 25, 26

N

networks 102
nested lists 23
NotebookDirectory[] 35

O

OpenStreetMap 119

P

PairedBarChart 80
PairedHistogram 80, 84
ParallelTable 27
partition function 30
periodic patterns
in time series 50, 51
PieChart 86
plot
about 34
isocontour plots, preparing 72
styling 39-41
PlotLegends option 41
PlotRange property 37
plotting functions
3D point plots 43, 44
legends 41, 42
ListPlot 36-38
log plots 44, 45
PointLegend 41
PolarAxes option, SectorChart function 55
PolarGridLines option, SectorChart function 55
PolarTicks option, SectorChart function 55
position function 31

protein molecule, visualization
about 67, 68
interactivity, adding 73, 74
isocontour plots, preparing 72, 73
isosurface plot 74, 75
loading 69-72
manipulate, using 74, 75

R

rainbow color map 125
RandomVariate function 85

S

scalar field 12, 13
scientist, visualization 76, 77
SectorChart function
about 54, 57
options 55, 56
PolarAxes option 55
PolarGridLines option 55
PolarTicks option 55
SectorOrigin option 55
sector charts 51
SectorOrigin option, SectorChart
function 55
select function 30
SetDirectory[] 35
SetDirectory function 35
set operations
applying, on lists 29-31
show command 62
similarity maps
about 89
for smaller datasets 92-94
SmoothHistogram 80
statistical, visualization
about 80, 81
appropriate plots, selecting 88, 89
charts 82
high-dimensional data 89
Histogram 82
swiss bank notes dataset 81
StringSplit function 99
styling 74, 75
SwatchLegend 41
swiss bank notes dataset 81

T

table 12
table entries
with multiple elements 25-27
tally function 30
text 15
text, visualization
about 96
code 99
explanation 100, 101
word cloud 97, 98
time series
about 14, 49
periodic patterns 50, 51
visualization 49
visualization survey, URL 77
Total. Total function 33
tuple 22

U

union function 30

V

visualization
about 8
demonstrating 9-11
deploying 127
further readings 20
significance 9

W

webMathematica interface 127
word cloud
about 97, 98
basic algorithm 98
data, cleaning 98
wrong distance metric
employing 94, 95

Thank you for buying
Mathematica Data Visualization

About Packt Publishing

Packt, pronounced 'packed', published its first book "*Mastering phpMyAdmin for Effective MySQL Management*" in April 2004 and subsequently continued to specialize in publishing highly focused books on specific technologies and solutions.

Our books and publications share the experiences of your fellow IT professionals in adapting and customizing today's systems, applications, and frameworks. Our solution based books give you the knowledge and power to customize the software and technologies you're using to get the job done. Packt books are more specific and less general than the IT books you have seen in the past. Our unique business model allows us to bring you more focused information, giving you more of what you need to know, and less of what you don't.

Packt is a modern, yet unique publishing company, which focuses on producing quality, cutting-edge books for communities of developers, administrators, and newbies alike. For more information, please visit our website: www.packtpub.com.

Writing for Packt

We welcome all inquiries from people who are interested in authoring. Book proposals should be sent to author@packtpub.com. If your book idea is still at an early stage and you would like to discuss it first before writing a formal book proposal, contact us; one of our commissioning editors will get in touch with you.

We're not just looking for published authors; if you have strong technical skills but no writing experience, our experienced editors can help you develop a writing career, or simply get some additional reward for your expertise.

Python Data Visualization Cookbook

ISBN: 978-1-78216-336-7 Paperback: 280 pages

Over 60 recipes that will enable you to learn how to create attractive visualizations using Python's most popular libraries

1. Learn how to set up an optimal Python environment for data visualization.

2. Understand the topics such as importing data for visualization and formatting data for visualization.

3. Understand the underlying data and how to use the right visualizations.

MATLAB Graphics and Data Visualization Cookbook

ISBN: 978-1-84969-316-5 Paperback: 284 pages

Tell data stories with compelling graphics using this collection of data visualization recipes

1. Collection of data visualization recipes with functionalized versions of common tasks for easy integration into your data analysis workflow.

2. Recipes cross-referenced with MATLAB product pages and MATLAB Central File Exchange resources for improved coverage.

3. Includes hand created indices to find exactly what you need; such as application driven, or functionality driven solutions.

Please check **www.PacktPub.com** for information on our titles

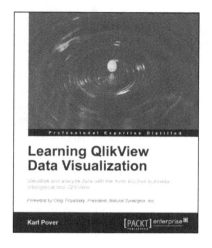

Learning QlikView Data Visualization

ISBN: 978-1-78217-989-4   Paperback: 156 pages

Visualize and analyze data with the most intuitive business intelligence tool, QlikView

1. Explore the basics of data discovery with QlikView.

2. Perform rank, trend, multivariate, distribution, correlation, geographical, and what-if analysis.

3. Deploy data visualization best practices for bar, line, scatterplot, heat map, tables, histogram, box plot, and geographical charts.

Data Visualization with D3.js Cookbook

ISBN: 978-1-78216-216-2   Paperback: 338 pages

Over 70 recipes to create dynamic data-driven visualization with D3.js

1. Create stunning data visualization with the power of D3.

2. Bootstrap D3 quickly with the help of ready-to-go code samples.

3. Solve real-world visualization problems with the help of practical recipes.

Please check **www.PacktPub.com** for information on our titles

www.ingramcontent.com/pod-product-compliance
Lightning Source LLC
Chambersburg PA
CBHW082121070326
40690CB00049B/4026

9 781783 282999